The Great Multinational Tax Rort

Martin Feil was born in 1947 in Sydney. While attending university for 13 years (10 years part-time) on a scholarship, he got his first job in the Customs department, and then became the Tarriff Board's youngest project director at the age of 26.

He was eventually responsible for 11 major industry inquiries, before striking out on his own and working as an industry-policy consultant for the next 30 years. During that time he also owned trucks, warehouses, customs bonds-stores and container yards, and worked for the Australian Taxation Office as one of the few Australian independent experts on transfer pricing and profit repatriation by multinationals. He has been chairman of the Institute of Chartered Accountants' customs committee, and the institute's representative on the tax office's transfer-pricing subcommittee.

Feil has written many op-ed pieces over the years for *The Age*, accompanied by illustrations by John Spooner, warning of the dangers of free-trade ideology. He is also the author of *The Failure of Free-Market Economics* (Scribe, 2010).

The Great Multinational Tax Rort

how we're all being robbed

Martin Feil

Scribe Publications
18–20 Edward St, Brunswick, Victoria 3056, Australia
2 John St, Clerkenwell, London, WC1N 2ES, United Kingdom

First published by Scribe 2016

Text design by Mike Kuzsla
Typeset in Garamond Premier Pro 12.5/17pt

Printed and bound in Australia by OPUS Group

Scribe Publications is committed to the sustainable use of natural resources and the use of paper products made responsibly from those resources.

9781925321647 (Australian edition)
9781925228908 (UK edition)
9781925307856 (e-book)

CiP records for this title are available from the National Library of Australia and the British Library.

scribepublications.com.au
scribepublications.co.uk

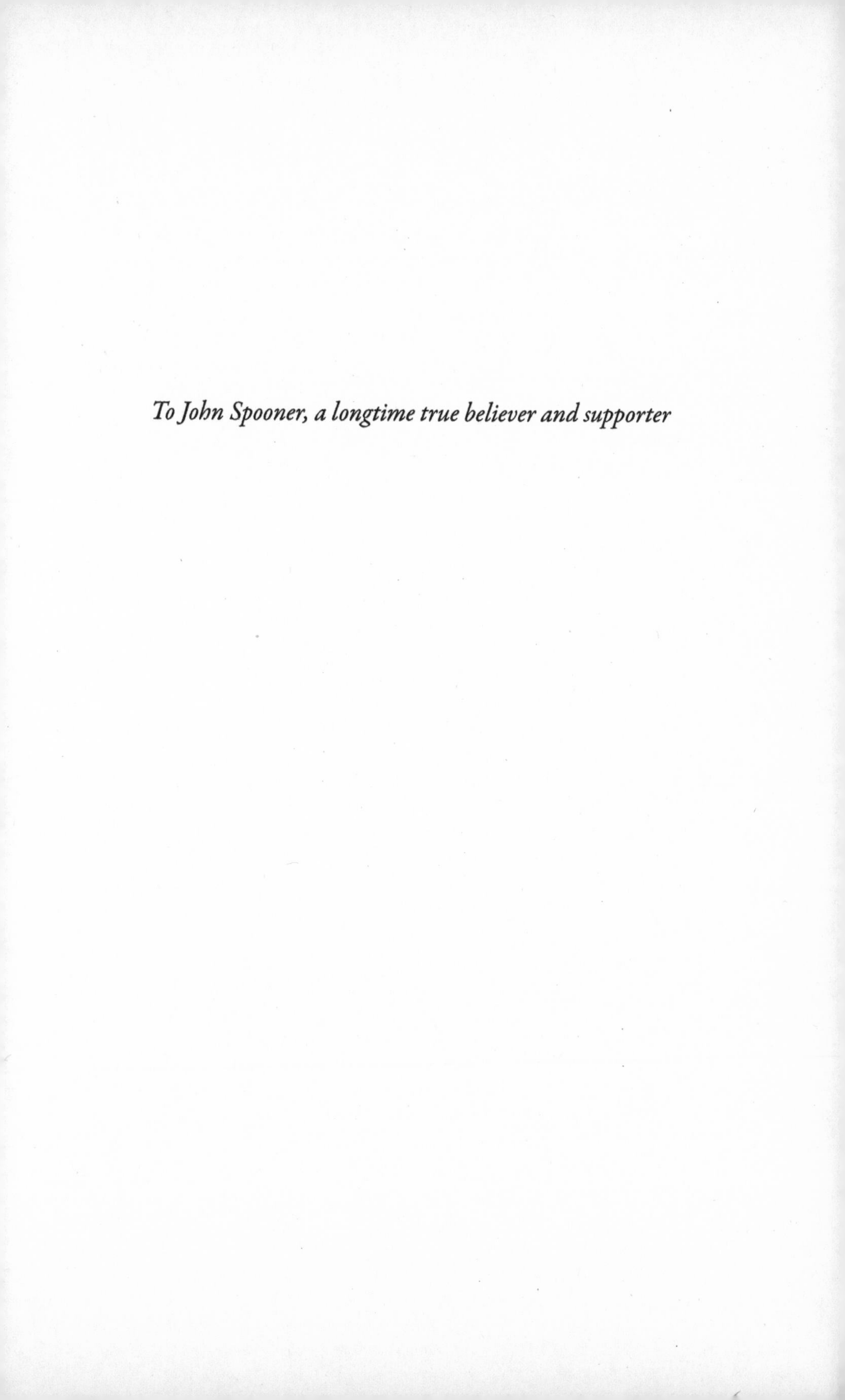

To John Spooner, a longtime true believer and supporter

Contents

Appendices

Preface

This book is not about the Panama Papers. The 11.5 million pages released in the first tranche of those documents revealed truly shocking global tax avoidance and tax evasion — but they dealt with the behaviour of wealthy individuals and their tax advisers. They did not deal with similar behaviour by multinational corporations and their very highly paid tax advisers. The latter is a much bigger problem, and it is what this book is concerned with.

Panama has been known as a tax haven for more than half a century — one of at least 70 tax havens throughout the world, including the British Virgin Islands, Gibraltar, Jersey, the Seychelles, the Isle of Man, a number of ex-British Commonwealth countries, and Delaware in the United States.

The total number of tax havens isn't known, but it is estimated they are holding between $21 and $70 trillion on behalf of high-wealth individuals. In his 2015 book, *The Hidden Wealth of Nations*, the economist Gabriel Zucman calculated that 8 per cent of the financial wealth of households, or $7.6 trillion, is held in tax havens, and that the money hidden in those havens causes a loss to global tax revenues of US$200 billion a year — including $35 billion in the US and $78 billion in Europe.

A large number of such havens have existed for at least 100 years. Until the Panama Papers, governments had turned a blind eye to their existence and function, taking care not to press the havens to obtain information about the identity of account-holders. The one possible exception to this behaviour was the Nazis, in the course of their theft of massive amounts of artefacts, art, gold, and other treasures of Europe during World War II. It is likely that some of that treasure is still held in the tax havens, if only because the passwords that would enable their withdrawal have been lost.

The Panama Papers. were exposed by an unprecedented leak from an unknown source to the German newspaper *Süddeutsche Zeitung*, which went on to share them with the International Consortium of Investigative Journalists. The documents came from the database of the world's fourth biggest offshore law firm, Mossack Fonseca, which acts for 300,000 companies — more than half of which are registered in British tax havens, as well as in the United Kingdom. It is the worldwide revelation of the beneficial owners of those offshore companies — including many wealthy and highly placed people in a number of countries — that has led governments to start working out what actions they can or should take against their citizens and the tax havens they use.

Transfer pricing is a completely different matter. This technique, developed by multinational corporations, has been out in the open for at least the last 25 years, with more and more devastating consequences for governments and their citizens around the world. The multinationals have perfected the practice of selling to their global affiliates at prices that would send the affiliates bankrupt if they were left on their own, trying to recover their inflated import costs in the marketplace. The affiliates survive only because the banks of the world lend them money based on surety letters from their parent companies or regional head offices.

This process has allowed multinational firms to dominate the markets for goods and services in around 180 countries, or to operate without permanent establishments and to have no tax obligations anywhere. This trick relates principally to internet operators such as Google, Amazon, Apple, etc, and to 'sharing-economy' companies such as Uber and Airbnb.

There are approximately 500 multinational companies in existence, who control about 60 per cent of world trade, and whose brand names are familiar to the media and the population. Most of the world's major economies are members of the Organisation for Economic Cooperation and Development, and have participated in its major meetings in Paris over the last two years, where the core problems caused by transfer pricing have been clearly expressed and discussed. As a result, the governments of many major economies have recently subscribed to a level of mutual tax cooperation that has never been previously known.

In 2013, the powerful UK House of Commons Committee of Public Accounts received evidence from the Big Four accounting firms' subsidiaries in the UK. The report it issued, *Tax Avoidance: the role of large accountancy firms,* was damning:

> HM Revenue & Customs (HMRC) appears to be fighting a battle it cannot win in tackling tax avoidance. Companies can devote considerable resources to ensure that they minimise their tax liability. There is a large market for advising companies on how to take advantage of international tax law, and on the tax implications of different global structures. The four firms employ nearly 9,000 people and earn £2 billion from their tax work in the UK, and earn

> around $US25 billion from this work globally. HMRC has far fewer resources. In the area of transfer pricing alone there are four times as many staff working for the four firms than for HMRC.

The parliamentary report effectively expresses the UK government's position on transfer pricing, and is discussed at length in Appendix F. Their estimate of lost revenue is immense. Partly as a result of this, the HMRC is consulting on a set of draft rules to ban tax-avoiding businesses from being awarded government contracts. That would be devastating for the companies, but hasn't even been raised as an issue in Australia.

The quantity of the tax revenues being denied to governments around the world by transfer pricing is unknown, but occasionally snippets of information emerge that hint at the enormous size of the losses. For example, the UK pharmaceutical firm AstraZeneca was found in 2015 to have paid no tax on £3 billion of profits, after having channelled funds through a subsidiary in the Netherlands. And a recent report from the UN Conference on Trade and Development has revealed that, in 2015, multinationals funnelled £221 billion through low-tax jurisdiction such as The Netherlands, and through tax havens in the Caribbean.

To some extent, the Panama Papers. have been a distraction. Outing high-wealth individuals may create an interesting circus, but it is not really the main game.

Introduction

International trade began over 2,000 years ago, and is the oldest element of the global economy. In many ways it has been responsible for the prosperity, security, and happiness of the vast number of people lucky enough to be living in the developed world.

In the twenty-first century, international trade has metastasised, and now reaches a global population of many billions of customers, including impoverished people in the most isolated and undeveloped of countries. The dominant suppliers are multinational corporations that have few competitors other than each other.

Until the end of the twentieth century, most manufacturing nations created barriers regulating the entry of imports. The barriers included customs duties, quotas, import restrictions, and non-tariff measures. The 'Protection Wars' ended in the last decade of the twentieth century.

The modification of national border protections has created a global trade environment misnamed 'free trade'. Together with free-trade agreements (which are not free, either) governments have completed a series of bilateral and multilateral agreements that provide a measure of entry into markets (though only for some goods) that were previously impenetrable. So far, no major national market is completely free of either tariff or non-tariff protections.

These political moves have had little impact on the strategies that multinationals use to penetrate and dominate virtually every national market of substance.

The weakening of border protection resulted in another kind of foreign invasion. When *ad valorem* tariffs (based on percentages of import value) were reduced, import prices rose. High customs duties had previously been a deterrent for multinational parent companies charging prices that, together with duties and marketing on-costs, could not be recovered in the consumer market by their subsidiaries.

The multinationals' light-bulb moment was to recognise that subsidiaries did not need to make a profit in every national market. In fact, foreign governments would want to collect taxes on any such profits. The multinationals' solution was to impose charges on their subsidiaries for royalties, manufacturing knowhow, and technical-service fees. There were no taxes on charges for intangible services. These parent-company imposts ensured that the subsidiaries never made a profit and so never paid company tax. In some cases, the subsidiaries incurred losses for decades.

The almost meaningless expression 'transfer pricing' is used to describe the pricing mechanisms that multinationals employ to charge their subsidiaries in overseas markets for the subsidiaries' purchases of goods and services, intellectual property, interest on loans, and much else. These charges, usually excessive, are imposed where the parties to the transaction are related by common ownership: that is, where it is a parent–subsidiary relationship. The subsidiaries have no choice in the transactions. Those prices would not be acceptable (they would, indeed, be ruinous) to an arm's-length purchaser, as they do not enable the purchaser to on-sell the goods, intellectual property, or services at a profit.

Years (or even decades) of continual losses by a multinational marketing affiliate, for instance, indicate that the parent company is not charging an arm's-length price for goods, services, and intellectual property. Some subsidiaries of multinationals have not made a profit in over 20 years of operation in Australia. No business operating on its own behalf continues in business if it makes a loss year after year, unless it is contributing to an international profit across borders. Banks do not lend to independent companies that make such losses.

Generally, the purchaser is wholly owned by the parent, though it may simply be controlled by a much lower level of external ownership. This level of 'controlling' ownership varies from market to market. And although the ATO accepts that start-ups will often make losses for two or three years, losses over any longer period are a clear indication that a multinational affiliate is not acting at arms' length.

Multinational ownership and control does not rely on a single shareholder owning 51 per cent of a company's shares. A 10 per cent ownership can be enough to control a company, through disciplined voting of the bloc of shares on major issues, and the broad distribution of remaining shares to a large number of shareholders.

Governments need tax. The decline in income tax, company tax and, in Australia's case, a stubborn bipartisan political refusal to increase the GST to the levels that are common in Europe, will ultimately mean that national governments will not be able to meet the social and infrastructure-development obligations that they were elected to deliver. The problem is the mismatch between the demand for government services and the supply of tax revenue. Demands upon the public purses of all government authorities are increasing, while tax collections are falling relative to the increasing size of national populations.

Although the full-blown blight of transfer pricing has been with us for 25 years, it has been a known and growing threat for much longer. In a special message on taxation to the US congress in April 1961, President John F Kennedy said:

> Recently more and more enterprises organised abroad by American firms have arranged their corporate structures aided by artificial arrangements between parents and subsidiaries regarding intercompany pricing, the transfer of patent licensing rights, the shifting of management fees and similar practices ... in order to reduce sharply or eliminate completely their tax liabilities both at home and abroad.

We don't often think much about tax. It is one of those subjects that you know has an impact on your life but you are not really interested in. Maybe you don't want to know. Tax usually gets taken out of your wages or salary, and you get what is left.

Alternatively, you may own a small business and have to pay a number of different taxes, including company tax. You either struggle with the end-of-year return to the Australian Tax Office, or get an accountant to help you. Either way, it costs you time and money.

This book explains how multinational corporations have avoided trillions of dollars of tax over the past 25 years. That number is not an exaggeration. They don't 'evade' tax; they 'avoid' it. Tax 'avoidance' is legal, but tax authorities will try to collect the additional tax and impose a charge for the period of time they are out of their money. Tax 'evasion' is illegal and, if the case is serious, the tax office may try to send the offenders to jail.

Multinational corporations generate profits in around 180 countries around the world. They work hard to avoid, reduce, or delay their tax obligations for as long as possible, and they generally succeed. Sometimes they pay nothing or, at best, the percentage of their multibillion-dollar incomes they pay in tax is a lot less than the percentage an individual worker pays.

Four accounting firms — PricewaterhouseCoopers, Ernst & Young, KPMG, and Deloitte — are the global accountants and tax advisers for the multinationals. They have been paid over $500 billion in the past 25 years to prepare annual accounts and to manage the multinationals' tax affairs. The favourite tool of the 'Big Four' accountancies to minimise tax for their multinational clients is transfer pricing: a complex and confusing array of methodologies and strategies that works to reduce tax or even avoid tax payments altogether.

This book explains how transfer pricing developed, and describes the strategies and tactics that the Big Four global accounting firms use.

The negative financial and economic impact of this behaviour on the nations of the world is about a lot more than just money. It strikes at the heart of how governments obtain the financial resources they need collectively to make global society function efficiently and compassionately. That goal demands a fair taxation system in which everyone contributes according to their ability, and receives support from government according to their needs.

Governments need taxes to pay pensions, build infrastructure, and provide services, and help those who can't help themselves. In particular, most people do not believe in ignoring the poor, the old, the helpless, and the underprivileged.

According to a report issued by Oxfam in April 2016, tax dodging by multinational corporations costs the United States approximately US$111 billion each year. A follow-up report in June 2016 by Oxfam Australia found that, in 2014, an estimated $638 billion worth of multinationals' profits had been shifted to tax havens, resulting in $172 billion of tax revenues being denied to 110 developing countries, preventing crucial investments in education, healthcare, infrastructure, and other forms of poverty reduction.

The French-born economist Gabriel Zucman calculates that more than half of the foreign profits of US firms are booked in tax havens. Zucman puts the annual tax-revenue losses of this practice at $130 billion — even more than Oxfam's estimate. According to Zucman, the effective tax rate paid by US corporations has been reduced by one-third since the late 1990s. Other reports indicate that Apple, for example, had an effective tax rate of 1.9 per cent on its US$36 billion of international earnings in 2012.

The Organisation for Economic Cooperation and Development (OECD) is the peak tax and economic advisory body for most major countries. The good news is that it is at last slowly coming to accept that it must act to put a stop to multinational tax abuse. At the G20 conference in Lima, Peru, held in October 2015, OECD secretary-general Angel Guerra said: 'The G20 has recognised that BEPS [base erosion and price shifting] is eroding the trust of citizens in the fairness of tax systems worldwide, which was why we were called on to prepare the most fundamental changes to international rules in almost a century.' (Base erosion and price shifting is a technical term referring to the negative effect of multinationals' tax-avoidance strategies on national tax revenues.)

For the last 30 years, the ATO has attempted to deal with transfer-pricing issues on a basis of confidentiality of interactions with major multinational taxpayers (including audits that last for many years, and advanced pricing agreements). It has negotiated compromise outcomes with those major multinational firms, their parent companies, and their home tax jurisdictions involved in correlative relief. The ATO has also issued a large number of transfer-pricing rulings to explain its view of the law.

This softly-softly approach has had limited success. The OECD's direct major engagement in 2014, and the support of the G9 and the G20 in 2015, has raised the bar for concerted action by a number of major economies.

The 2015 Australian Senate inquiry into corporate tax avoidance and minimisation also shone a light on the impact of transfer pricing — in particular, on the pharmaceutical industry, where companies that had not directly engaged the ATO paid single-figure tax rates, while similar companies that had done so paid tax rates of the order of 30 per cent. Their products were often similar. The subsequent release of outstanding major company tax-obligation data by the commissioner extended the debate into the public arena.

In 2014, the ATO initiated a major review of 180 multinational affiliates that had undertaken base-erosion and profit-shifting strategies that had the impact of reducing their Australian tax obligations and capturing the benefits provided in low-tax jurisdictions. A deputy commissioner, Mark Konza, was given the responsibility of managing the BEPS review, which involved the provision of $180 million in additional funding to the ATO. That major review is still in progress.

Konza's boss, Chris Jordan, the ATO's commissioner, has recently become a prominent and blunt critic of the multinationals' tactics and behaviour. In early 2016, he criticised them for deliberately thwarting Australia's tax-collection efforts, and told the senate inquiry that, 'Their clear tactic is to delay and obstruct. They game the system. Enough is enough.' He said he was sick of being 'stooged' by companies refusing to provide information in time.

Jordan also leads the Joint International Tax Shelter Information and Collaboration network, of which the UK is a leading member. At a meeting in Paris in early 2016, chaired by Mark Konza, it resolved to develop a global approach to the exchange of information on tax collection.

It's only a start, but finally the penny has dropped.

Part I
Setting the Scene

CHAPTER ONE

What's the trouble with multinationals?

This book is not about tax, accountancy, and economics — the academic disciplines and the sources of the tools and strategies involved in what is emerging as the greatest human and financial disaster that the world has ever known. This book, instead, is about the outcomes of the deliberate business decisions of many intelligent, highly educated, industrious, experienced, and wealthy people who are the leaders of major businesses in most of the world's larger economies. The problem has come from a direction that no one expected, and has been created and developed by people whom most of us respect and, in many cases, admire.

Those people own or direct the policies and strategies for major businesses and brand names, or they work for the business owners who belong to the richest group of people in the world.

The owners of multinational corporations and brand names (which includes their shareholders) and their accounting and legal advisers should be leaders and helpers showing and teaching the people of the world how to improve their lives. These corporations and these people have the money, the history, the education, the talent, and the power to lead. They own virtually all the global patents of brand-named consumer goods and services.

Despite this wealth, the multinationals have not led as they should; in fact, they have gone in the opposite direction. They have had a negative financial impact on the world economy and global society. For the past 25 years, virtually all multinationals have refused to pay a fair share of tax relative to their incomes, by employing what are known as transfer-pricing methods and strategies, and by using tax havens and/or artificially domiciling their businesses in low-tax countries.

In the past 25 years, many multinationals have been involved in audits, disputes, threats of litigation, and litigation with national tax authorities that have lasted for anywhere between five and 15 years. The final tax settlements reached between the multinationals and the tax authorities have often been less than half the tax, penalties, and interest payable amounts calculated in major position papers by those same national tax offices after years of audit.

Such stonewalling greatly enhances the multinationals' ability to compete in and dominate their markets. Although sometimes there may be more than one multinational in the same national market, they usually avoid potentially damaging open competition. There are, of course, exceptions, and some multinational feuds have lasted for decades.

Virtually all multinationals manufacture their products in China and other low-cost countries, in the process often trashing their domestic competitors with imports. Yet the savings they make through their transfer-pricing tax strategies and by manufacturing in low-cost countries are not passed on in full to their customers through lower retail prices. These practices have created major damage, and threaten the quality of life of a substantial part of the world's population.

The multinationals' strategy is to produce consumer goods

with globally known and enormously valuable brand names (which they own) at the lowest cost (often in undeveloped or developing countries), and to sell them for the highest possible price in developed countries. They are generally the only supplier of a brand name.

These tactics have been strengthened by the creation of global purchasing groups (owned and directed by the multinationals and brand-name owners), which source intermediate products from low-cost countries (where they often own the means of production and are in partnership with governments), and add value in other countries before final marketing and distribution. Global manufacturing and purchasing groups reduce the opportunity for manufacturers in resource-rich countries to add value to raw materials, create scale economies, and increase their own wealth by moving up the production chain and reducing transport costs.

The development of global supply groups has been lauded as a great efficiency by the Organisation for Economic Cooperation and Development (OECD). But it is actually a beggar-thy-supplier practice wherein the multinational often demands efficiency dividends every two years from the manufacturers, whether manufacturing cost-reductions can be achieved or not. The OECD needs to take a closer look at how these global supply groups operate. In particular, it should look at the margins allowed by the multinationals in each step in the global supply chain.

In the twenty-first century, manufacturing has become a developing-country activity. China is the world's factory. Its global competitive advantages are the ability to pay its labour force very little and to not be constrained by unions or considerations of the environment or factory conditions.

China and other Asia-based manufacturers have annihilated much of the competition from other countries for basic textiles, clothing, and footwear, and for a broad range of consumer goods. They are also fast becoming the world's supplier of more up-market products and dirty products such as lead-acid batteries.

From the perspective of the Reserve Bank of Australia, the World Bank, and the OECD, there is a new explanatory theory for Australia's decline in manufacturing. A 2013 article by Gerard Kelly and Gianni La Cava, two staffers at the Reserve Bank, explains the concept of global supply chains in glowing terms.* For them, supply-chain cost improvements are all that matter. Social consequences are 'exogenous variables' in the efficiency equation. (That is, their value is determined by factors outside the causal system of their study.) The World Bank and OECD have also praised the opportunities created by global supply chains.

The theory fits well with the globalist philosophies of many upwardly mobile staffers in the internationalist banking sector and major government policy organisations such as Treasury, the Reserve Bank, and the Department of the Prime Minister and Cabinet. They are usually born and educationally bred internationalists. They are generally not strugglers from the working class. Virtually all the Reserve Bank assistant governors in Australia completed their educations in economics at Harvard. That has been a Reserve Bank tradition. Its senior people have never worked anywhere other than at the Reserve Bank.

In July 2014, the OECD published the first part of a 'Report to the G20 Development Working Group on the impact of BEPS on low-income countries'.† BEPS is 'base erosion and profit shifting'.

---

* 'Value-added trade and the Australian economy' (*RBA Bulletin*, March quarter, 2013, pp 29–37).

† (www.oecd.org/tax/part-1-of-report-to-g20-dwg-on-the-impact-of-beps-in-low-income-countries.pdf)

The report provides a very different perspective from that of the Reserve Bank authors, who do not seem to consider the working conditions or income of the workers. The OECD authors observe that profit shifting through supply-chain restructuring that contractually reallocates risks and associated profit to affiliates in low-tax countries is an obvious outcome when global supply chains are owned by multinational corporations.

A further practical problem that the Reserve Bank and other academic proponents of global supply chains do not mention is the impact created by the enormous extent of customs-duty reductions in most manufacturing nations over the past 30 years. The connection between that process and the rise of transfer pricing has not yet been discussed in academic papers.

It is unlikely that Customs officials in any country would closely examine customs-valuation issues, given the fact that duty rates on goods being moved offshore and further processed or manufactured in the global chain are now very low (or non-existent), and that the interpretation issues for cross-border goods-tariff classification and customs valuation are often complex.

A substantial proportion of semi-manufactures moving along a multinational manufacturing supply chain is held and further manufactured in one of the world's 3,000 free-trade zones. It is likely that Customs authorities would not even look closely at the electronic documentation that might be held in the zone. There is no socially beneficial purpose arising from revenue payable to the national location of the zone, as the goods never enter home markets.

Looting a country of its resources and paying the local citizens risible amounts is an old invaders' trick that still works well in the twenty-first century. Australia is a perfect contemporary example.

I wonder if the Aztecs and Incas agreed when the Spaniards took away their gold. The Aztecs and Incas dug the ore up and refined it, but the Spaniards sailed away with the final product. The South American economies never recovered from the loss. Their descendants have always been poor. The Aztecs and Incas felt the long-term impact of global supply chains.

Australia is the source at the beginning of a global supply chain in precious metals, minerals, and petroleum gas, and a variety of other raw materials. Our role in the chain is to grow, dig, or pump up the iron ore, coal, gold, and other metals, petroleum gas, foodstuffs, and other basic commodities (particularly wheat and wool), and deliver them to ports for export aboard foreign ships with foreign crews. This functional description sounds a lot like that of the Aztecs and Incas.

We have followed a national strategy of supplying a narrow range of exports for a very long time. Australia has exported greasy wool for nearly two hundred years. We have been supplying gold for a hundred and fifty years. We leave it to other countries to make gold products from our gold, and fine suits from our wool. China (with the benefit of the ownership of patents and intellectual property, assistance on quality control, and supply of manufacturing knowhow) adds value to raw materials sourced from all over the world to create manufactured goods for the world. Australian raw-materials exports are increasing while further-manufactured final products and intermediate goods are declining rapidly.

Australia is a resource-rich economy that will ultimately have no resources left. If you fly over Western Australia, you can see the scars in the earth from iron-ore mining, even when the plane is at an altitude of 10,000 metres.

If we look into the recent past, BHP used to be a world-class steel producer with a range of products that matched that of the Japanese steel industry in the 1960s. Essington Lewis, the company's managing director at the time, boasted that BHP produced every type and shape of steel that the Australian market needed. In the twenty-first century, the company is a shadow of its former self. In the 1970s, BHP was the largest company in Australia and employed over 70,000 people. Most of those men were migrant labourers. There is little work for them now.

In the last half-century, the multinationals and global owners of brand names and intellectual property have learned the lessons of rigorous quality control and brand management. They have embedded these techniques in offshore factories in China and other low-cost manufacturing locations. Even many luxury products are now manufactured in China. All that these manufacturers have to do is receive the manufacturing knowhow and quality-management intellectual property from the brand-name owners, and follow scrupulously the detailed manufacturing processes. They are given the technical advice necessary to ensure that the product meets specifications, and the value of the brand name is protected. They can then move back in the supply chain to source the lowest-priced materials or components that meet the quality standard.

They pay a royalty or other intellectual-property and knowhow fee to the owner of the intangibles. These fees, however, are not arm's-length prices.

If the greater part of the world's supply of consumer goods is provided by companies directed or owned by multinationals, the question is whether this is an outcome which is to the benefit of society. Global experience suggests that it is not. Multinationals are avoiding their tax obligations and hollowing out the domestic infrastructure of local supplier industries in smaller or poorer countries that used to have substantial basic manufacturing sectors. The movement of components, intellectual property for components assembly, and other supply-chain services are major opportunities to implement transfer-pricing strategies.

Contrary to the opinion of the Reserve Bank staffers, and despite the applause of many academic economists, global supply chains have a major downside, because they are a principal way of avoiding tax obligations through BEPS. In those circumstances, the base erosion occurs in the switch from taxable local transactions to transactions in trade zones that are not subject to the duties and taxes of the countries where the multinationals reside. The Reserve Bank staffers, moreover, are unlikely to be aware of the detail and technicality of the customs practices for valuation and classification of goods internationally traded that have existed and been discussed and modified internationally since the end of World War I.

When imported goods are further processed in a free-trade zone and then exported without entering home consumption, no cross-border taxes are payable. Showrooms, transport, and storage are features of free-trade zones, so marketing can occur and goods can be sold before the goods are entered for home consumption. There is no warehousing of duty-paid goods, nor any carrying duty and GST/VAT imposed for the interval between the cross-border arrival of the goods and their sale to customers. There is no need for export entries.

The world's greatest weapons of mass economic and social destruction

Warren Buffett (once the richest man in the world) famously said that 'derivatives are weapons of mass financial destruction'. He was right. Derivatives are even-money bets. Someone loses and someone wins, every time. Nothing is created or developed. It is the biggest casino the world has ever known, and produces nothing. Sixty trillion dollars is bet in this casino every month. *Forbes* magazine estimated that the total global trade in derivatives is $US700 trillion. That is 10 times the global national income of $US70 trillion.

Transfer pricing is an even more dangerous weapon of global mass financial destruction. And the only winners are the multinationals. Transfer pricing allows multinational corporations that do not want to pay tax to retain practically all their profits. For the last 25 years, this hidden tax strategy has significantly reduced the tax paid by the businesses that control 70 per cent of the world's trade in goods and services.

The trouble with transfer pricing is that it has already metastasised and spread throughout all economies that trade internationally. This financial cancer was deliberately introduced more than 25 years ago by multinational corporations that didn't want to pay the amount of tax they were obliged to pay (but were able to avoid or delay for years, without commensurate penalties or interest on late payment) in each of the 180 national jurisdictions where they, their subsidiaries, and their affiliates operated as manufacturers and distributors.

Global legal practices and the Big Four global accounting firms (Deloitte Touche Tohmatsu, PricewaterhouseCoopers, Ernst & Young, and KPMG) already knew about tax havens and tax treaties, and used them for their major wealthy clients. Transfer pricing provided a new opportunity to pay little or no tax. Tax treaties always involved paying some tax. Tax havens, with their ultra-secretive practices, have gained the opprobrium of national governments. Lose the password or die, and you or your heirs will have no access to your account.

Originally, there were eight global accounting firms (the Big Eight), and they were responsible for the multinationals' taxation and other financial returns to the tax authorities in each country where a subsidiary was located. Since then, the Big Eight firms have been reduced to four, and these Big Four earn more than $US100 billion a year in transfer-pricing fees alone. It is their most profitable revenue stream.

Transfer pricing also provides the global opportunity for 'correlative relief'. This is another obscure expression that means nothing to most people. It refers to the fact that, in circumstances where goods and services have been imported at prices above the arm's-length price, it is likely that the Treasury of the exporting country has received taxes paid using the value of an inflated export price. The mutually agreed solution by OECD member countries is that the exporting country will refund to the exporter the tax difference between the transfer price and the agreed arm's-length export price charged to a subsidiary. This sounds (and is) fair, but those foreign treasuries are very slow to disgorge the tax payments they should never have received in the first place. Instead, they bargain with the tax authorities who were short-paid taxes for years. Again, the outcome is a settlement that doesn't ever match the amount overpaid to the tax authorities at the source of the export.

Essentially, the OECD's transfer-pricing process of resolution ultimately enables enlistment of the Treasury of the multinational's sourcing country as an ally of the multinational. A negotiated retrospective decrease in the import price of goods and services means that tax was overpaid in the exporting country. That tax is refunded in total or part by the tax authority of the exporting country. The argument about the refund settlement can cause a delay of years before the final resolution of the dispute. Tax treaties always involve a lower tax, and also complicate tax settlements.

The strategies of the hugely compensated Big Four accountants are not the only cause of this tax-avoidance problem. Other generously compensated participants include tax havens — which hold more than $30 trillion — and the lawyers who interpret and negotiate tax treaties between nations. The havens are the ultimate destinations of tax-free funds in or near major nations. They include the state of Delaware in the United States, Bermuda, Panama, Liechtenstein, Luxemburg, and Jersey in the Channel Islands, and larger countries such as Switzerland, Ireland, and Holland. (For a longer list of tax havens, see Appendix C.)

Large national legal firms are also involved. They have been the advisers and legal draftsmen who have created and negotiated the abundance of tax treaties that are a major adjunct to transfer pricing. Country-to-country treaty tax rates are substantially lower than most domestic company tax rates.

Tax officers in individual countries cannot compete with the teams of Big Four advisers that virtually all multinationals employ. After all, the multinationals possess the enormous financial resources accruing from their vast share of global trade.

National governments cannot afford the social welfare and other services their citizens expect if they do not collect substantial taxes from the wealthy users and beneficiaries of their societies and their domestic markets. Overcoming this global tax problem and its eradication will take decades. This is not an even-money bet, as with derivatives, where there is an equal winner for each loser. We all lose. Even the multinational cannibals will starve eventually when they collectively beggar their customers and their societies.

Apart from transfer pricing, the other major part of the problem arises from multinational manufacturing, mining, and purchasing in developing countries or in China. There is obviously a substantial financial benefit to the multinationals in doing so. The question is, though, what global social cost (including the cost to the developing countries' and China's workers) is being paid by making China and other low-cost countries the world's manufacturers?

The multinational strategies shouldn't be about grinding widows and orphans in Dickensian style. They shouldn't be the twenty-first-century exploiters of the poor in developing countries, whom they pay subsistence wages in factories and mines that often do not meet safety or environmental standards. The multinational business model is to buy and produce cheaply; maximise profits; and then pay no tax (or very little) on their profit. Ultimately they will cannibalise their own markets because consumers won't be able to afford their products. The entire population of Australia can't get unemployment benefits from Centrelink.

Australia has been called the Lucky Country. How long will our luck last in the face of a strategy that will ultimately beggar nations and annihilate tax receipts? This is an era of an ageing population (the baby boomers) in an industrialised mature economy. The boomers will expect government support as they grow older and more infirm.

The defining question for the future is, how can the nations of the world make multinational corporations pay a fair share of their income in tax? That is the conundrum that the OECD faced in Paris in 2014. The strategies and concepts the OECD has developed (in conjunction with the G9 and the G20) will be put to the test over the next few years. (See Chapter 13.) Even so, a total resolution may take decades. Transfer pricing won't be easily eradicated from the world economy.

Doing nothing is not a viable alternative. The outcome of that strategy as it has been employed till now is evident in the risible amounts of tax that virtually all multinationals have been paying for the past quarter-century.

CHAPTER TWO

The games the Big Four play

Tangible goods have been traded between nations at least since the Phoenicians began exporting to Rome in 400 BC. They sold a purple dye that Roman senators and nobles used to distinguish their rank by the coloured band on their togas. This dye was possibly the first internationally traded commodity to be recorded.

Soon, Rome was importing from Roman provinces and foreign nations a range of luxury goods and delicacies that were not produced or previously available in the homeland.

The Romans also imported services in the form of the slaves who worked on and managed their estates and households. Greek slaves ultimately ran the Roman Empire while the Romans behaved badly. The great innovation of the Graeco-Roman government bureaucracy was to tax the imports. Trade between countries was a new empire (and global tax opportunity), and it became the cornerstone of civilisation.

International trade has come a long way since 400 BC. It grew from domestic markets in which merchants walked with their produce and animals to nearby castles and towns. Eventually their goods were loaded aboard sailing ships trading with the East Indies. These ships were funded in shares by the merchants themselves. The British occupation of India led to the creation of a trading empire that included India, the West Indies, Africa, and the Spice Islands. Britain's cotton trade with the southern states of America made those states rich before the American Civil War.

The world of trade has also come a long way in logistics. The constant growth and technical development of cargo transport internationally has been one of the great pillars enabling the creation of a global economy.

Global trade between nations has enriched our lives and improved the standard of living for the people lucky enough to live in developed countries. The supply chain has gotten shorter and shorter. And, of late, import duties and quantitative restrictions have virtually disappeared.

But the greater part of the world's population lives in undeveloped countries. They didn't win the lottery of birth. Many now seek (as did the English, the Irish, the Germans, the Italians, the Lebanese, and the Greeks when they came to Australia in the 1950s and 1960s) to migrate to the lucky developed countries of the West. There, they live happily themselves, and raise their children with a standard of living that their parents could scarcely have imagined.

However, international trade in goods and services has been dominated by multinational corporations in the past few decades. This dominance is a threat to the lifestyles and social welfare of those peoples who live in (or who have recently migrated to) developed countries. Their lifestyles and hopes are threatened by a long and debilitating global multinational crisis (GMC).

The GMC is a threat to most of us. It will blight migrant aspirations and, to an extent, the lifestyles of those who have already reached their new homes in other countries and have created families. In these times there is no longer the range of opportunity for upward, social, and financial mobility that existed in the past. Unless governments can collect sufficient tax, the standard of living of the great majority of their citizens will fall to unacceptable levels.

Governments must have tax revenue to conduct the management, social-welfare, and education programs of the nation. These are the programs built up in the interests of the great majority of citizens. They don't depend upon the occasional philanthropic whim of the super-rich.

If you believe that the global financial crisis (GFC) of 2007 caused long-term social damage and destruction in the world economy, you should be aware that the GMC has already been much more destructive than the GFC, and has lasted much longer. It has grown to a malignant maturity that threatens to destroy (and has already eroded) the tax base of major, mature industrial economies over the past 25 years. Multinational corporations are also directly exploiting the people of small, developed economies (such as Australia) and developing economies. The GMC is still evolving and will continue to stunt the growth of the world economy and damage the quality of life of the vast majority of the world's people, unless the OECD, the G9, and the G20 can develop a concerted strategy to curtail the effects of the malignant greed that has possessed the multinational corporations.

This situation is no accident. It is the outcome of a decades-long strategy developed and employed by the multinationals and their financial advisers. Their goal is to pay as little tax as possible in every market where the multinationals have a subsidiary company. The main strategy to this end is what is known as 'transfer pricing', which was developed in the late 1980s and early 1990s.

Every affiliate of every multinational in every economy of substance now uses these tax-minimisation strategies as a matter of course. (Previously, multinationals had developed their affiliate strategies and conducted their tax affairs on a country-by-country basis.) Yet it was not until 2013 that national tax authorities and international organisations collectively set about challenging these techniques for profit shifting and transfer pricing.

Virtually all multinational parent companies and their affiliated manufacturers, marketers, and distributors throughout the world pay negligible company tax (generally less than 10 per cent of their income) in any of the 180 countries where they operate. No nation's company tax rates are that low. Many are in the 20 to 30 per cent range, while some countries (such as Russia) have higher rates. For some of the multinationals, a zero or single-figure tax rate is their goal. These corporations would regard their Big Four tax advisers as second-rate strategists if their advice resulted in them paying more tax than a single-digit percentage.

This is obviously an antisocial, destructive attitude that national governments cannot afford to tolerate indefinitely. But how long will they wait? The authorities have undertaken many tax audits and reviews, and reached many settlements over the past 20 years. But the audit process is inefficient and lengthy. Nor does it ever recover enough overdue tax to be worth all the effort, and the penalties it imposes are never stiff enough to induce the multinationals to change tactics.

Transfer pricing directly saps the ability of national governments to fund their essential functions: to provide aged care, education, border control, transport infrastructure, roads and rail, hospitals, and the myriad welfare programs that a modern nation requires. Broad-based personal income tax cannot generate sufficient revenue to fund the essential activities and social commitments of the modern welfare state, especially as it deals with an ageing population that lives longer. Customs duty collections are no longer a substantial contributor to state coffers.

The tax paid by a large part of the population that used to be employed in manufacturing has been eroded in relative terms. A decline from 27 per cent of the Australian workforce to 8 per cent simply cannot be explained by saying (as the Productivity Commission did) that the workers have migrated to more competitive industries and higher-paying occupations in the supply chain. Most of them have not. Many of the displaced workers couldn't get a job (particularly if they were middle-aged), and went to Centrelink. They now rely permanently on unemployment benefits.

For 30 years, the Productivity Commission gave a series of explanations for the employment shift in Australia. The commission no longer asserts that the displaced workers in manufacturing migrated to more competitive and efficient industries. It has gone quiet on that idea.

The substantial rate of increase in both state and federal government social and health-care commitments as the Australian population ages is a looming financial and social disaster. Treasury forecasts for health and aged-care expenditure in the next 20 years indicate that Australia urgently needs company-tax payments (at the rates passed by parliament) from multinationals, and income-tax contributions from high-income earners, to balance the national budget.

The Big Four accountancy firms will dismiss these forecasts as in error, extremist, or alarmist, or will simply ignore them. Perhaps they should respond by disclosing the tax/income algorithms they have used for 25 years and their analytical justifications for ignoring the OECD's core methodology of the comparable uncontrolled price as a way of determining the correct arm's-length price for the sale of tangible goods between related parties.

The Big Four's clients and their subsidiary affiliate/marketers-distributors operate in around 180 national markets selling global brand-name products that either monopolise a market or compete lethargically and carefully with one or two other global competitors. Strategically, they don't enter very small national markets except for mass consumer product sales. Publicising the weighted average company tax rate on profits paid by global companies with revenue above a billion dollars would be enlightening for both tax authorities and the public in general. The Big Four might explain why they believe the major governments of the world are wrong when they have vocally criticised (through the G9 and OECD) the actions of the Big Four to help their clients minimise their tax obligations in the countries where they live, work, and make money. That is not the usual relationship between governments, major institutions, and powerful companies.

Some of the global companies (especially technology and internet companies that have no physical establishment in most or all markets) have been exposed recently in the media for paying no tax at all. A few of them have responded by volunteering to pay relatively trivial amounts of tax, at least in the United Kingdom. This is disgraceful. Income and business taxes are not gifts to the nation. It is not the same as giving a tip to the doorman at a hotel where you have stayed for a while and intend staying again. The attitude seems to be that the amount is trivial, but it is good politics to be friendly to those who look after you.

The global banks have been a great help to the multinationals. They are the conduits and facilitators of the multinationals' transfer-pricing tax-minimisation strategies. And they provide financial facilities to companies that, to go by their balance sheets, have not made a profit for decades.

Multinational corporations should pay most of the world's

company tax because they are the beneficiaries of most of the consumer and company revenue at every level of retail sales in every substantial national market. As we have seen, they are responsible for more than 70 per cent of the world's trade in goods, intellectual property, and services. They use the infrastructure of our cities and towns — they just don't want to pay for it. In Australia, company tax is usually levied only once a company achieves an income threshold. It is not borne by Australia's very small businesses.

Until now, legal practitioners and judges (other than those judges adjudicating transfer-pricing cases in the UK's House of Lords) have largely remained aloof from the melee. The legal fraternity in the major industrial economies have long-standing client relationships with multinationals, but their clients only deal with them when there is a potential legal conflict or business acquisition/disposal opportunity. Lawyers generally wait for customers to come through the door, rather than acting, as the Big Four does, to provide an unending and internally related stream of advice and opinion. Such intimacy between companies and their auditors may be a mistake in the long run.

As the public becomes more aware that many major companies pay little or no tax, these companies' lawyers should be concerned enough to talk to internal legal counsel and any senior board members who are concerned for their personal probity and integrity. Senior counsel within multinationals in the US are jealous guardians of their corporate and brand reputations, and of the public's attitude towards their brand names.

Part of the growth of the Big Four has been a consequence of the Australian legal profession's lack of interest in transfer-pricing disputes. Chief Justice Murray Gleeson (who occupied that important office in the High Court of Australia for 10 years and retired in 2008) typified that lack of interest. Chief Justice Gleeson expressed the view that the High Court should not consider tax cases; he believed that they should be litigated and resolved by lower courts of appeal. Given the number of intermediate courts that plaintiffs and respondents have to go through to get to the High Court (and the likely expenditure of millions of dollars), that attitude is understandable.

Seven years is probably about the standard time taken from beginning a disputed matter in a lower court and receiving High Court decisions in a major case that can be funded by both parties Then, even after winning the legal case, the winner's costs and the losing side's costs are usually taxed to arrive at a lesser amount. The final amount returned to the successful litigant seldom covers its actual costs. That amount does not include any payment for the successful party's executive review time, for example. These payments are not even partially recoverable. They also often include large amounts spent on a senior counsel's opinion on the chances of success based upon a brief by senior solicitors before the client even decides to proceed to litigation.

Few companies would proceed if they believed they were headed to the High Court. This would involve obtaining several positive lower-court decisions, seeking leave to appeal to the High Court, and then appearing before the court itself. The time and cost involved in going through this process is one reason why overseas litigation funders have become more prominent in legal actions, particularly in class actions.

The legal profession's attitude may change now, given the recent global criticism of the Big Four and the latter's intrusion into the legal market for treaties through the creation of their own legal practices. It is a pity the lawyers didn't enter the transfer-pricing market a quarter-century ago.

It must be appreciated that a major barrier for the lawyers is the fact that they share clients with the Big Four who are also an important source of work, especially in relation to legal opinions (although the Big Four now often brief counsel through lawyers in their own legal practices). So it is no surprise that the legal firms are leery about approaching the Big Four's clients directly.

The lawyers' interest may be piqued when the Big Four become legal competitors in well-funded, major legal cases such as the *Chevron v the Australian Taxation Office* case (at present in the Federal Court), where the Australian Tax Office (ATO) is demanding payment for retrospective tax on cross-border transactions dating back to 2004. (See Appendix B.) These cases will involve decades of legal work and matters of great principle. Neither party will terminate the action if it loses in the first instance.

The multinationals employ only the Big Four to prepare their complicated and large annual returns (which have to be prepared in 180 countries, and involve additional returns for domestic subsidiaries). The multinationals' rationale in this is that it ensures a global consistency of approach, analysis, and transfer-pricing methodology. Equally, this ensures that the Big Four keep their clients for decades. The audit-knowledge transfer required to change accounting firms is too daunting, dangerous, and expensive — though some will eventually have to make some shift in the US, given recent legislation there.

The Big Four provide continuing advice on tax issues (both domestic and international, as well as often-called 'controversy advice') for the multinationals, and have moved into several other disciplines, especially involving mergers, disposals and acquisitions, state government consultancy and economic advice, and representation for national governments and their clients. They have acquired significant economic consultancies. The Big Four also dominate the global market for a range of other accounting and advisory services, including special government audits, floats, economic analysis, and reports by parent public companies to shareholders, and audits for state government authorities and public-private partnerships.

Audit has been the traditional financial heart of the relationship between the Big Four and their multinational clients. The Big Four provide the revenue and expenditure scorecard in annual accounts for the multinationals at the end of each financial year. And the Big Four audit and tax partners are 'on call' as sources of advice and conduits between the ATO and multinational affiliate and parent companies (wherever the parent companies may be located physically).

Transfer-pricing analysis should be a literacy rather than a numeracy discipline. In most cases, functions, assets and risk analysis can't be completely explained or justified solely by numbers.

The determinative reason for the relative absence of legal advisers in the transfer-pricing debate is that legal practices are not usually international partnerships. European, US, Japanese, and Korean multinationals all use the Big Four's European affiliates. When transfer pricing began, its great sales theme was that all affiliates 'would sing from the same song book'. This meant that a multinational was able to impose a standard philosophy and discipline of accounting strategies upon its affiliates that was based on best-practice accounting (from their perspective), that had global board approval, and that was based on the best available international accounting advice. It also meant that there was no conflict between the accounting treatment of subsidiaries from country to country.

This global strategy is very cost efficient and is supported by multinational funding that simply isn't available on a country-by-country basis. It is cost effective because all affiliates use the same accounting methodology.

Australian lawyers have not yet developed or tested the necessary transfer-pricing knowledge and skills sets that they will need in transfer-pricing court cases to enable their virtually unchallenged use as precedents in court proceedings.

Until the Chevron case in the Australian Federal Court began in 2014 there had been only two transfer-pricing cases that went to court in the previous 20 years in Australia. (See Appendix B.)

The Chevron case is a major litigation test based upon contentious retrospective tax legislation that allows the ATO to reopen audits a decade (or more, as the years of litigation and hearings in intermediate courts pass) after it closes a case. This dispute in principle probably will not be finalised for almost a decade. And a lot of other companies will find themselves in the ATO's litigation queue if Chevron ultimately loses. If Chevron wins it will be a bad defeat for the ATO, and will make other retrospective claims much less likely, despite the legislation. The judicial reasons for the decision will be critical.

Chief financial officers working in multinationals and their major affiliates often spend the early years of their accounting careers at one of the Big Four. The usual management practice in Australia has been to send young accountants (who look to the partners to be likely candidates for ultimate partnership) to either Europe or the US, so as to have rising young executive contacts within the major parent companies that they deal with. They are also likely to meet senior partners and rising stars in the European and US practices that have relationships in the multinational's head office. The partners I met at Deloitte in London in 1991 were outstanding. I was told that the Dutch practice was even better. It had 6,000 staff.

All the Dutch partners received the same income, but such egalitarianism wasn't even contemplated in the Australian practices. In the early days of Deloitte, the partners' agreement stipulated that a major unanticipated fee (that is, not an audit fee) meant that the partners who marketed and earned the fee could receive as much as 5 per cent of the partnership income. The agreement didn't say 'net income'. That clause was enshrined in the partnership agreement for a long time, and it caused a lot of bitter disputes. In 1990, for example, the insolvency partners at Deloitte had completed some major receiverships (including Conrad Black's purchase of Fairfax). Five partners marketed and completed the assignment. The rest of the partnership of 80 partners didn't get much individually that year. Some of them had earned more as managers.

Those who didn't become partners were often placed in strategic clients' accounting divisions, and became their finance directors. They were generally regarded as having been schooled in the appropriate Big Four defensive responses to queries or audits of multinational accounts emanating from tax authorities and other government financial institutions. They seldom became managing directors.

These selection strategies for audit rising stars are no longer as relevant as they were 20 years ago. Because of the sheer volume of highly paid work for a large number of staff in transfer-pricing assignments, this has displaced audit as the major power within the Big Four.

There is a lot to be said for major legal firms establishing a coherent understanding of the issues resulting from transfer-pricing audits and reviews, but they are never part of the initial analytical process. It was common for the major legal firms to become involved only when a dispute between the accounting advisers and the multinational was likely to go to court, but that doesn't happen so often now. The legal issues are initially dealt with by the Big Four's internal lawyers, who select and brief counsel. That change occurred in the 1990s, and probably fractured relationships between the lawyers and the accountants to some extent.

Second-partner reviews of advice to clients are common enough among major accounting firms, but a junior partner would have to feel very confident about his or her opinion to contradict the senior partner, especially if the conclusions of the initial review had already been conveyed to the client.

No country, other than the United Kingdom, has much of a history of tax-scheme litigation. Lawyers (and judges) generally rely on precedents. The UK cases are about the tax schemes used prior to the birth of transfer pricing, but much of the logic applied to the issue of artificiality has general intellectual veracity. Many of the UK's Law Lords' decisions and their reasons are brilliantly expressed and logically argued.

There are few contemporary precedents in transfer pricing in Australia, but that will change — and the pace of change will quicken — in the next few years.

The most common transfer-pricing method used globally is the transactional net margin method (TNMM.) This is the method used in at least 90 per cent of transfer-pricing reviews. It is relatively simple to use, but can be easily applied in a self-serving fashion. There is a tremendous temptation to pick a comparable example with functions, assets, and risks that assist the client's analysis when shopping for arm's-length comparables.

TNMM is an accountants' and statisticians' lightweight solution. So far, it has not succeeded when exposed to the glare of judicial scrutiny in Australia's higher courts.

The enormous fees ($500 billion in the last 20 years, according to the UK parliamentary committee of inquiry) that the Big Four have received for their transfer-pricing work is an indication of the universality and substance of the damage that corporate global tax avoidance has caused to the revenue collections of the world's economies in the past 25 years.

CHAPTER THREE

Base erosion and profit shifting

> BEPS relates chiefly to instances where the interaction of different tax rules leads to double non-taxation or less than single taxation. It also relates to arrangements that achieve no or low taxation by shifting profits away from jurisdictions where the activities carrying those profits take place.
>
> Pascal Saint-Amans,
> director of the OECD's Centre for Tax Policy

Base erosion and profit shifting (BEPS) is OECD-speak for the strategies that multinational corporations have used to re-characterise and hollow out their commercial and marketing activities in countries where their subsidiaries have previously been core marketers and distributors of product.

To give a prominent example, Australia Post is a partner with a foreign multinational in what is possibly the largest BEPS strategy in Australia at present. That strategy is in relation to internet-based purchasing of foreign consumer goods. The overseas suppliers of these good are often affiliates of major multinationals (especially in the clothing, footwear, cosmetics, toiletry, and fragrance industries). Internet purchasing now constitutes 15 per cent of the Australian retail market, making it the largest consumer goods market in the country.

Australia Post distributes imported, individual retail purchases, and its business was considerably enhanced by the Australian GST-free threshold of $1,000 for goods bought over the internet. The dominant overseas door-to-door delivery service in Australia is provided by the ex-German post office, DHL. The company was floated on the German stock exchange 25 years ago, and is now one of the world's largest employers, with over half a million drivers, logistics managers, and other staff.

Australia Post is a willing, subordinate partner of DHL. If the DHL couriers don't find people at home to receive a delivery (and they often don't), customers must pick up the parcel at the post office. Very little time is spent by couriers at the delivery address. This is a major flaw in the practice. Consumers don't consider the cost of time and disruption involved in them becoming part of the supply chain themselves when they either wait at home or have to make a visit to the local post office to receive their purchases.

BEPS poses a serious risk to tax revenues and national sovereignty. David Bradbury, Australian assistant treasurer in 2012–13, said in March 2013, 'It's a threat to our sovereign right to tax and to raise the revenue necessary to provide the public goods and services our society requires.'

In absolute terms, base erosion and profit shifting can be regarded as having begun in Australia in 1990, when most manufacturing activity began to be moved offshore by its multinational owners. The Australian media applauded the process of hollowing out the manufacturing sector. Their conclusion was that manufacturing workers were lazy and inefficient, and deserved everything that happened to them. This view ignored the motivation to reap the tax advantages and cheap labour of BEPS.

Yet as BEPS has risen in use in Australia, accompanied by the fall of tariff barriers, at no time has the Productivity Commission (or the Industries Assistance Commission before it) bothered to recommend that duty savings should be passed on (as they were with sales tax) to the consumer. This indifference or ignorance has had a catastrophic impact on the Australian economy.

Multinationals may introduce BEPS in a piecemeal fashion over years or even decades. They tend to be mindful of their reputation with consumers who have been customers for decades. For instance, all the departed or departing car manufacturers from Australia have established reputations for their marques that will resonate in the imported-car market for decades.

The BEPS strategy is simple enough. The brand name is established in the market, with substantial assistance from the government. The barriers to importing competitors are high and, in some periods, insurmountable. To return to the example used earlier: in the 1980s, the use of quotas, Australian design rules, and a 57.5 per cent customs duty meant that the then four major Australian car makers supplied almost 80 per cent of the market.

BEPS may begin with moving call centres to low-labour-cost countries. The functions so moved are then gradually broadened to include finance, maintenance, repairs, property management, and marketing functions. In some cases, the back offices become regional head offices reporting directly to the parent company for all issues involving the subsidiaries.

As we have seen, one damaging BEPS outcome in Australia has been to reduce manufacturing's contribution to GNP from about 27 per cent in the 1970s to 8 per cent now. Yet the car importers that are subsidiaries of the major car companies will be able to keep their tax losses and increase their global profitability.

An early example of BEPS at work is the fate of Australia's textiles, clothing, and footwear industries, which disappeared 20 years ago. Local manufacturers once employed over a million people, including over 200,000 people in each of those industries (and a similar number in the car-making industry). Today in Australia, textiles, clothing, and footwear is only a wholesale and retail marketing operation, although some illegal sweatshops exist. The wholesaling and marketing functions are substantial, but are not led by Australian companies. They are controlled by Chinese entrepreneurs, whose relationships are mainly with Chinese manufacturers.

Australia's standard of living, income levels for workers, and income-tax system make our manufacturers uncompetitive. Our real competitive disadvantage is that we have not followed the lead of our Asian neighbours and allowed tax-free repatriation of income earned overseas and a flat 10 per cent tax on income earned in the Australian economy. How can you beat that if you still want to provide the social services and unemployment safety net that Australia provides to its citizens? These do not exist in Singapore or Hong Kong. Australia's largest government institution (Centrelink) provides welfare to the aged, the sick, the needy, and those who did not provide for their old age. However, Australia's approach is not a common government policy globally.

Throughout the Asia-Pacific region, there is competition to be the location of multinational hubs. These hubs employ tens of thousands of educated workers from several countries. Singapore led the way 30 years ago in offering incentives to multinationals to establish regional head offices there.

Consider this matter politically. What would the local workers and companies in Australia think if our government offered attractive tax terms and incentives to foreign workers and foreign resident companies? We would end up with a two-tiered society that follows the Asian model of guest child-minders, cooks, and cleaners with limited civil rights who are carefully monitored and ultimately returned to their home countries.

(This has, in fact, occurred to a limited extent here. Consider the 457 visa system for foreign workers in the mining and agriculture industries, where Australian workers simply can't be found. These workers live in rural and mining outposts. The workers lack acceptable housing and other public infrastructure, and often share beds if shift work is involved. The practice has become something of a scandal, as unions have kicked up a stink over pay and conditions and the fact that foreigners are taking Australians' jobs.)

Such practices are much more widespread in Singapore, Hong Kong, Dubai, and some of our other Asian neighbours. Of course, those countries don't provide the same aged-care, health, and education assistance to the guest nannies and other workers that we do to our older and poorer citizens. They are sent home after a few years. Equally, of course, the Asian economies don't provide the same level of social services, unemployment benefits, health, aged care, or wages to those who aren't talented, educated, or industrious. Medical and dental costs in Singapore, for instance, are horrendously high.

In Asia, many multinationals have established regional offices responsible for the business carried on in several countries that charge no tax for income earned abroad. And usually the host country has only a 10 per cent rate for income earned there.

Tax havens are the other major revenue-holding locations that multinationals use, but it may be that low-tax countries are the best long-term tax-reduction option. Given the long-term existence of some tax havens and the amount of money in them ($US20–30 trillion) on which no tax at all is paid, they must make tempting targets for tax-starved countries. However, tax havens may not divulge any information to foreign tax authorities, although these are now putting depositors under ever-greater pressure. These tax authorities are aware of the multinationals' sales and earnings within their jurisdictions, and often have a good idea of where the money goes.

Low-tax countries such as Hong Kong and Singapore are attractive alternatives to havens for regional head offices, as they offer a lifestyle for their thousands of staff that simply does not exist in the morgue-like silence of the havens. They neither manage nor grow the money. They merely mind it.

BEPS is the cornerstone policy that annihilated Australia's manufacturing sector. It has a long history in Australia, where its growth has been accompanied by the fall and ultimate irrelevance of Australia's tariff and non-tariff barriers. That reduction to irrelevance was engineered by the Productivity Commission, and it left Australian manufacturing with no protections. Australian tariff and non-tariff forms of assistance are now the lowest in the world, apart from the tax regimes of the Asian entrepots and sheikhdoms seeking guest workers and to attract the regional head offices of major businesses.

In plain language, BEPS involves moving the major functions (apart from some marketing and back-office functions that can't be done on the internet) of subsidiaries marketing consumer goods from a taxing economy to low-wage and low-tax countries. This migration of functions may occur in a piecemeal fashion over a number of years. Australia's car industry is a great example.

The most successful BEPS strategy in Australia has been implemented by a coalition of interests including multinationals, the media, the universities, government departments, and the Productivity Commission. These have worked together to persuade successive federal governments to implement policies that have reduced the contribution of manufacturing to Australia's gross national product (GNP) from about 27 per cent in the 1970s to the present level of 8 per cent. To give one major industrial tariff-reduction example: overseas carmakers have directly benefitted from a reduction in customs-duty rates from 57.5 per cent in the late 1980s to 5 per cent in 2015.

The result has been the almost complete closure of our motor-vehicle manufacturing industry. Only Ford remains, and even it plans to leave. But even if Ford wanted to stay, it would eventually lack the critical mass of local components manufacture that every carmaker needs to be viable. The cascading skills and employment losses in the components and after-market industries are also consequences of BEPS.

Over the next few years the Australian motor-vehicle components industry, which once consisted of over 200 companies, will be devastated and eventually disappear. Some of the larger suppliers are subsidiaries of multinational component manufacturers (Bosch, for example). Many of them, however, are Australian companies with no overseas markets. And here there is no non-tariff assistance regime for them, as exists in Europe and Asia for local manufacturers.

Meanwhile, Qantas has moved its maintenance activities to Singapore. This represents the erosion of a major activity of this Australian industry icon (which began in the 1920s) that obviously is a much more strategically and financially important function than back-office and regional management functions. The question in the Australian people's minds is whether future maintenance will perpetuate Qantas's proud boast that it has never had a major air accident since it began operations in the 1920s.

After manufacturers, the next major Australian companies most at risk from BEPS are the large retailers in major shopping centres. They have no alternative overseas opportunities, so their closure will be extremely costly for shareholders and employees. They are the major players in an industry that employs more than 200,000 young people, mostly women. Even now, many customers only visit these stores to check out colours, sizes, and styles, and then buy the garment, shoes, cosmetics, or perfumes on the internet. The internet shopfronts don't pay tax or provide the working conditions that the major retailers provide. They have no permanent establishment in Australia, so they are not taxable. How long can the major Australian retailers compete with this?

Australian retail mark-ups on imported cosmetics, toiletries, and fragrances are often some hundreds of per cent, so there is plenty of opportunity for high market penetration by offshore-based internet retailers.

Internet shopping is growing rapidly. It is a classic child of BEPS. Virtually all internet income is going offshore, and even small domestic internet shopfronts in Australia are not paying company or any other Australian indirect tax, including the GST. Many would be paying no income tax.

For years, the country's GST-free internet threshold of $1,000 for a single transaction ensured that for 99.9 per cent of imports bought over the internet, there was no duty or GST payable. As an importing business, you could have a hundred $800 transactions a day at Australian ports. The $1,000 figure was by far the highest internet threshold in the world, with the only exceptions being the revenue-duty items of alcohol and tobacco. The threshold had been maintained since the introduction of the GST, but in 2015 the mounting loss of tax revenue finally led the Commonwealth and the states to agree to reduce the threshold massively. The new law takes effect on 1 July 2017, at the same time as the so-called Netflix Tax comes into effect, finally applying the GST to foreign companies selling digital goods and services into Australia.

Why do multinationals use transfer pricing? I suppose it is like the short-term madness and hubris on Wall Street that created the global financial crisis. There seems to be no end to greed, even if it is ultimately terminally destructive for the greedy. The owners and senior executives of the great global brands have already made an enormous amount of money. Yet they seem to want more. The Big Four accountants and economists involved in transfer pricing are also, even by their standards, making a great deal of money.

Transfer pricing may have been the sort of gradual development that can go unnoticed in the early stages of a new tax paradigm. In the early days of transfer pricing (1990), there was no self-serving complexity in the analysis, the choice of methodology, or the dealings with the ATO. The Big Eight's original task was to use the OECD methodologies and functional analysis to reach the best outcome derivable from the arm's-length data available in relation to their clients' cross-border transactions with affiliates. There was no apparently deliberate intention to make the analysis so complex that it couldn't be understood by tax officers, or to obfuscate the facts and circumstances of the transfer-pricing activity by making comparisons that weren't comparable.

The transfer-pricing (BEPS) strategy was the main subject of meetings of major world governments that took place at the OECD in Paris in October 2014 and again in 2015. The ultimate resolutions may take a decade or more to be implemented. The G9, the G20, and the OECD have all discussed, agreed, and publicly stated that the major instruments of the BEPS strategy are causing major damage to company tax collections among national economies that are members of the OECD. These economies are the major contributors to the flow of goods and services worldwide.

The OECD announced measures to counter BEPS after the 2014 meeting, and these measures will have the support of all OECD countries. But will they be implemented? How long will it take to implement them? No doubt, exploiting inertia will be a major issue and a major strategy of the multinationals.

Can multinationals reverse BEPS? And, it needs to be asked, why should low-tax countries with attractive tax regimes that have been hugely successful in expanding their economies, and attracting clever and educated people to live and work there, reverse those strategies?

As BEPS involves moving offshore those functions of a business that do not have a physical, strategic interface with the market to lower-tax or to no-tax jurisdictions, it erodes the functions, assets, and risk foundation of enterprises in all major economies, and devastates the small feeder businesses that exist to supply services and goods to them.

BEPS enables huge cost and tax savings for subsidiaries (which have existed profitably in developed, taxing economies for almost 100 years, and which are moving part of their basic activity to a country that does not impose tax on income earned from overseas sales). BEPS may also enable business strategies that have no purpose other than to move payments offshore to lower-tax jurisdictions and, in some cases, to tax havens that impose no tax at all. Nor is base erosion limited to back-office functions. It can lead to the cessation of local manufacture completely; or it may only affect functions such as accounting, property management, records, payments to suppliers and governments, and other administrative functions.

CHAPTER FOUR

Treaties and havens

The OECD's role as custodian, creator, and modifier of the Model Tax Convention is, at least for some international traders and companies, more important than transfer pricing and BEPS. Those tax strategies were not on anyone's mind when the League of Nations met in Paris in 1921 to consider how the countries of the world could eliminate double taxation when goods and services crossed borders.

Europe (at Brussels) is also the home of the World Customs Organisation (WCO). That organisation resulted from meetings of European nations in 1951 that led to the harmonised tariff and customs-valuation principles that are used by nearly every country. The WCO has 179 members.

For more than 60 years, the OECD and the WCO have managed to create principles and perfect model documents and processes for the conduct of cross-border trade. But their standards of ethics, rationality, and disclosure are being threatened by BEPS and transfer pricing. There seems to be an implicit and certainly unjustified view among multinationals that it is reasonable — and certainly sensible — to pay as little tax as possible. That may be true when it comes to the construction of international tax laws, but transfer pricing and tax havens have gone well beyond that. The multinationals seem to have given no consideration to the social consequences of their strategies.

The OECD Model Tax Convention was last published on 22 July 2010. It is 2,134 pages long, and is constantly revised. It is a perpetual work in progress. There is a simple, single pro-social purpose in the document: to enable international traders of goods and services to avoid paying tax twice on the same goods and services. The Model Tax Convention achieves this by conferring an exclusive right to tax a transaction in the taxpayer's state of residence. Any other state that is a party to the cross-border transaction cannot tax that transaction. It has to allow tax relief, including for VAT or GST.

The same principle applies to the Harmonised Tariff and the Brussels Definition of Value, which enables importers in every member country to only pay duty once, and that at a percentage or fixed rate, or a combination of both. Customs and tax officers in the long-ago past took whatever they could get.

International traders in member countries of the OECD have the right to be taxed for each transaction in one country only. The principle does not apply to customs valuation, where a customs-valuation assessment is required in each country for raw materials, semi-processed raw materials, and intermediate and final products that move around the world from country to country, gaining value at each stage of process of manufacture, and ultimately being sold as finished goods in wholesale or retail markets.

From an international customs legislative perspective (in the context of cost, insurance, freight [CIF] valuation, which is the most common valuation system globally), value is added for customs purposes by every process of manufacture, movement, storage, and documentation in the supply chain for the goods. In each country in the multinational supply chain, the local customs authority is unlikely to know the destination of the finished goods unless the importers and exporters have arranged with them that the goods will be continuously documented along the supply chain, or the goods are at their penultimate destination.

In Australia, exporters and importers can claim back duties paid on goods (including semi-manufactured goods), or components, or materials within the exported products. Large importer/exporters often make such claims, but many smaller importers and exporters don't bother, as it is too difficult to track back through a series of transactions (with a mountain of associated documents) that are dutiable at rates of only 3 per cent or even zero. If an exporter could eventually get a refund of GST, it might change the equation. An increase in the rate of GST would certainly increase the attraction of refunds.

Managing the customs processes for global supply chains, and the consequential logistics (including electronic documentation) and tax and duty costs from country to country, putting the entire duty, VAT, and tax equation together, must be like playing three-dimensional chess.

In 2014, Australia was a signatory to 44 tax treaties. The treaty partners range in economic size from Malta to the United States, so treaties are obviously of global and enduring relevance for international financial transactions and the provision of goods and services. The basic concern is the offshore payment of dividends, interest, and royalties. Tax rates are negotiated between tax authorities on a bilateral basis, and they vary greatly. For example, dividend taxation rates may range between zero and 30 per cent; interest between zero and 20 per cent; and royalties between zero and 35 per cent. There are obviously large inequalities between countries in the extent of two-way trade and the benefit that each country perceives that it gets from the transactions.

Tax havens

The OECD has developed a 15-point BEPS Action Plan (which is dealt with in more detail in Chapter 13), several points of which are intended to deal with tax havens.

Tax havens may have some purpose that goes beyond reducing taxes *per se*. It is difficult, though, to fathom what that additional commercial purpose might be.

In any case, one of the methods of reducing tax is to move funds to places where both the national legislation and the implicit partnership of the authorities with the owners of the funds make it almost impossible to access the information that is necessary, within the law, to recover unpaid taxes and to prosecute those who established the arrangements. These practices are of long standing. Switzerland first became involved in these arrangements 100 years ago, when high-wealth individuals used them to hide their wealth from their home tax authorities.

Tax havens do not disclose to tax authorities either the source of their foreign holdings, or the companies or individuals who own or manage the ultimate ownership of the funds held in the haven. Havens shield income from all taxes. The paths of funds to the haven are generally unknown or obscured.

The most obvious and complete avoidance of tax globally has been achieved by companies operating entirely on the internet — thus having no permanent establishments — or using offshore conduits to tax havens for royalty payments that tax authorities have not worked out how to find and attack.

The best and most tax-effective havens probably haven't come to the attention of the global tax authorities. In some cases, several tax havens are used in the same money-movement transaction to obfuscate further the trail and increase the protection of personal information. A list of known tax havens is provided at Appendix C. Tax-haven users include major multinationals (and banks) in all the large economies of the world

According to Oxfam's April 2016 report, US multinationals such as Apple, Walmart, and General Electric have stashed $US1.4 trillion in tax havens. Overall, the use of tax havens allowed the 50 largest US firms to reduce their effective tax rate on $4 trillion of profits from the US headline rate of 35 per cent to an average of 26.5 per cent between 2008 and 2014.

Low-tax countries

Low-tax countries do make disclosures, but have globally accepted taxing mechanisms and rates that are much more competitive than those in most countries. They do not charge company tax on income earned outside the country, and charge a low rate of 10 per cent on income earned by individuals employed within the country.

The dollar-tax benefit of a multinational's moving its regional head offices to Singapore, Hong Kong, or other low-tax environments has never been calculated or publicly disclosed by any of the relocating multinationals, but it must be immense. However, this tax strategy is much more defensible than the strategy of actually hiding income in a tax haven. So it is unlikely in the present BEPS initiative that the OECD will put pressure on low-tax environments to change their tax policies. It would be difficult to apply any such pressure at this time, and doing so would be catastrophic for the low-tax environments.

It would also be resisted by many OECD member countries, many of whose nationals are employed in such environments — most notably in the United Arab Emirates.

The explosive development of multi-storey housing, offices, and city infrastructure in these countries is obvious. These nations are undergoing a revolution in their infrastructure growth, their accommodation of temporary migrant workers from all over the world, and their company-tax philosophy.

Twenty-first century Singapore is a revelation. I used to travel there regularly over 30 years ago, but only visited again in 2013. Some of the old colour, in places such as 'Boogie Street', has gone, but a lot of that will not be missed. Singapore is a beautiful place (especially near the water), and a dynamic global performer in shipping infrastructure.

Raffles isn't Raffles anymore. Before World War II it was the slightly rundown hotel home of traders in coconut oil and other exotic products from the islands of Indonesia and Malaya. The traders knew the area and the people. They became coast watchers and PT boat commanders in World War II. They told incredible but true stories about experiences such as attaching explosives to Japanese ships by paddling out to them at anchor in Singapore Harbour, or acting as coast watchers, radioing to Australia information on Japanese shipping movements. A client of mine at the time, Steve Stevenson (the original owner of timber importer Tenaru) was a coast watcher who managed to keep just one step ahead of a Japanese general who was on his trail.

Stevenson met the general in 1946 immediately after the war. The general laughed when he realised how close he had been to catching Stevenson. On one occasion, Stevenson had been hiding in a cave only 10 metres from where the general's troops were looking for him. The general enjoyed telling Stevenson what they would have done had they found him — they would have beheaded him.

After the war, traders such as Stevenson, based in Singapore, bought softwood timber plantations from the Dyak headsmen in what was then called Malaya. US interests were going to demolish the vast tracts of softwood timber for chewing-gum tree plantations. The timbers were Ramin and Meranti, which were soft woods that worked like hardwoods. They didn't warp like Pinus Radiata, and were a lot less expensive than the Douglas fir imported from Canada and Oregon in the US. Both timbers were used extensively in the Australian building industry.

The Australian timber-importing industry and timber merchants in those days operated the last of the supplier cartels in the world (in conjunction with US timber producers such as the giant Boise Cascade and Weyerhouser) in the Douglas fir trade that dominated housing structures. That cartel did not end until the introduction of the Australian Trade Practices Act in the early 1970s.

Today, Singapore, Hong Kong, and the United Arab Emirates provide major employment opportunities for millions of men and women from Indonesia, the Philippines, Bangladesh, Thailand, and Africa. The women work cleaning homes, cooking for families, and minding small children, in return for very basic incomes and living conditions. They live in tiny rooms, have Sundays off, and do the cooking, the cleaning, the ironing, and the grocery shopping. The men often live in camps, and work on major construction sites. They seldom leave the camps.

These days, all that is needed to be a strong economy on the infrastructure-development path is to have the ability to attract people from poor economies and to allow their employers to pay them a pittance. The income repatriated by Philippine women working overseas (mostly in Singapore and Hong Kong) is the largest source of the Philippines's export income.

The Singapore miracle is built on the foundation of a major

personal and business tax concession, and on a very industrious and clever people energised by the prospect of their major retirement benefits. In contrast, there is virtually no employment (and certainly no expatriate carer population) in tax havens. The central reason for their existence is to receive money and hide it from global tax authorities.

As we have seen, credible estimates of the amount of money held in 100 tax havens around the world range from US$20 trillion to $30 trillion. That is equal to approximately one-third of global annual income. To comprehend how much a trillion dollars is, consider the fact that Australia's present national income is about $1.4 trillion a year. That income supports the population of 24 million people. We have a relatively high standard of living, and substantial social security and health care.

The OECD's proposed reform of BEPS will not be achieved easily or quickly. Tax havens and tax-minimisation schemes have grown astronomically since World War II, yet tax authorities in major nations have been lethargic in response.

With the strategic advisory assistance of the global Big Four, major international legal firms, and the multinational banks, tax havens have finally achieved their intention. They hold trillions of dollars, and haven't paid any tax on either the principal or the interest that has accrued — over decades in some cases, where the original depositors must be presumed to be dead. Proving this may be an insurmountable problem for heirs seeking to obtain bank deposits made 70 years ago that they are entitled to. Even if the interest rates are in the small single figures, the interest and fees they have earned over time will be huge.

The question is, what's going to happen to that money in the future, or even in the present? What purpose will its existence serve, other than as a guarantee for global banks when the multinational directors seek funding for a dividend, a new company acquisition, or product development?

Tax deferral, and the fact that the corporation only ever pays a part of that tax (on the balance constantly held by the haven) are the primary purposes of these tax-haven deposits. Funds can materialise in years when profits are down and the share price needs a boost; or when there is an opportunity for insiders to buy shares; or when tax rates are low, and retained earnings can be used to create yet another subsidiary in an emerging market. Yet none of these tactics is in the interests of small shareholders.

There needs to be some explanation of how and why the multinationals' tax-minimisation strategy has been so wildly successful for them. Tax authorities may have been tardy in their resolution, but much of that is because of the correlative-relief process. Multinationals receive adjustments from overseas tax authorities when tax has been overpaid in another country because income was overstated on the arm's-length principle. These correlative-relief processes were developed by committees of country representatives in OECD meetings that lasted for decades. Member countries had to agree to any proposal unanimously. Disagreement meant that the country was expected to resign from the OECD. No wonder movement has been glacially slow!

The international correlative-relief process is the source of the common view that transfer pricing is simply a raid by one national treasury upon the revenues of another treasury. This may be partially true, but any alternative would be a policy nightmare. Completion of a transfer-pricing audit ultimately involves the consent to any arm's-length price determination by the tax authority of the country that is the source of the goods in question.

The fact is that the tax adjustments to the amounts multinationals have paid in their tax jurisdiction (the exporting country) is never anything near the amount of tax that they have avoided in the receiving country—which leaves the multinational disinclined, to say the least, to expedite any settlement with the receiving country. Conversely, nor does any overpayment in the exporting country ever come anything near to balancing the account. Settlements are always massively discounted. And the amount of time that tax authorities have to wait for payments is measured in years. In the meantime, the multinationals have the use of the money that they received based on transfer prices that were higher than the arm's-length price for the years during which the debate stretched on regarding the quantum of correlative relief to the taxpayer.

Time was when Switzerland was the only tax haven that most of us had heard of. A lot of cash is still held in banks there that dates back to World War II and earlier. After 70 years of compounding interest, immense fortunes must be waiting for the heirs to those long-ago-deposited funds left in safekeeping by their murdered grandparents, great uncles, and aunts.

Yet transfer pricing, BEPS, and tax-haven growth will be much more difficult to remedy and take longer to resolve than how to claim that money, or even how to counter the global financial crisis of 2007.

The overhang of the global financial crisis

In the last 25 years, the world economy has been visited by two self-induced financial plagues that, in all likelihood, will be more financially damaging and costly for the world than the two world wars. The consequence has been that the European Union is treading water and only a few member countries are in the black.

We are still living in a financial world damaged by the global financial crisis (GFC), and it exacerbates the transfer-pricing disaster. The GFC still reverberates in unemployment levels, home-mortgage rates, and bank-lending rates. Banks in Europe are offering rates of interest as low as zero per cent. They have been at record-low levels in Australia, and have created a housing-price bubble that is extremely dangerous. Interest rates are at zero in the UK.

The source of both the GFC and transfer-pricing viruses is the US. Few people have said this publicly, but it is true. A similar small number have criticised the government manipulation of exchange rates that gave the US an internationally competitive opportunity to trade out of the problem that Wall Street had created. The economies of the rest of the world were not strong. The US tactic meant that its devaluation of the dollar created a partial strategic path for the country to get out of the mess it had created by allowing NINJA (no income, no job, no assets) loans and snake-oil sales of securities globally at high interest rates that would never be paid. These securities will never mature. Most investors outside America lost virtually their entire investments. Legal cases in US courts resulted in foreign creditors receiving less than 10 per cent of their funds remaining after the debacle.

BEPS was already well established by 2007 (when the GFC began). It was always going to take many years to overcome the GFC. It is still reverberating in unemployment levels, and home mortgage and other asset losses, for millions of Americans.

Simply printing money during and for years after the GFC was good for the US, even though it was bad for the exchange rates and, consequently, for the terms of trade of other countries (including Australia) that traded with America. Does anyone believe, for example, that Australia's economy was so strong in 2011 that its dollar was really worth $US1.11? This artificial strategy made US imports dearer and its exports cheaper. The Aussie dollar rose, not because its economy was strong, but because the US central bank adopted a course of quantitative easing (that is, of printing huge quantities of dollars and devaluing the US currency). America's path out of the global crisis, which it had created, was to the disadvantage of the export trade of every other nation.

The strategy created major problems for every nation that wanted to export to the US. Their currencies were all relatively high against the US dollar, which effectively created a barrier against imports to the US, and made exports from the US more competitive.

A pertinent question occurs. What has the multinational corporations' decision to pay no tax or at best derisory amounts through transfer pricing got to do with manufacturing productivity and efficiency?

The greatest tax-minimisation strategy for a multinational probably lies in the unpaid accounts of its own subsidiaries. They don't have to pay for goods or services provided through their parent company, or regional office, or another subsidiary until it is financially strategic to do so. Nor do they have to pay tax on reserves that are not declared as income or profit. By contrast, no arm's-length business can be in constantly increasing debt over decades to its suppliers.

The question of late-payment interest arises also. Most affiliates do not pay tax unless it is strategically valuable to do so under the terms of a bilateral tax agreement with the country where its creditor affiliate resides.

Several of the OECD's BEPS Action Plan steps are intended to curb, to some extent, the operation of tax havens. Step 5 is the most relevant, as it involves countering harmful tax practices more effectively, 'taking into account transparency and substance'. (See Chapter 13.) Tax-haven practices are directly at odds with the pro-social principles of transparency and substance.

As we have seen, tax havens rely upon secrecy and a complete refusal to disclose their clients' holdings to tax authorities in other countries. They are not competitive with banks operating in the global market. They mind other peoples' money. They don't pay interest on it. They have no legal obligation to respond to the queries of foreign tax authorities. And the latter have no jurisdiction in the countries or islands where the havens are located.

Liechtenstein, Bermuda, the Channel Islands, Switzerland, and Delaware are examples of major havens that will not be closed down without a struggle, as they are aided and abetted by major nations. Following the money trail is a centuries-old occupation for tax authorities. Equally, it has been the occupation of many financial advisers on the side of those wealthy enough to want to hide their assets and income from the taxman. Tax havens do not have the pro-social justification that Singapore, Hong Kong, and other low-tax countries possess. They are not cost-efficient and globally competitive producers of electronics, pharmaceuticals, cosmetics, clothing, footwear, or high-technology goods. They don't produce anything.

Moreover, havens never operate as marketing or back-office functional hubs, or as regional head offices or call centres, or for any of the functions that are not directly involved in direct customer service or subsidiary management. Havens simply receive and store money that has come to them after a series of movements designed to throw tax collectors off the scent. Their job is to refuse to answer questions and hide the money. They live off the differential between the tax rate in the country where their clients generate taxable income and the environment in the tax haven where they pay no tax but do pay a service charge.

CHAPTER FIVE

Time is not of the essence

Time is the great enemy of the Australian Tax Office. The way it responds to the tax strategies of global businesses is lethargic and time consuming. The consequent costs to it of transfer-pricing audits are huge. The process needs to be simplified so as to reduce the time each valuation takes. The taxpayers — that is, the multinationals — keep their money until a demand is legally resolved. And even then they often get very favourable terms of settlement if a finding is made against them.

After the ATO completes a transfer-pricing audit, it presents its arguments to the taxpayer in a Position Paper. Thereafter the usual outcome is that the ATO proposes a settlement — generally for less than half the amount it has asked for in the paper, with associated penalties and late-payment fees. This avoids, for both parties, years of delays in correlative relief (which are generally reduced if the parties agree to a settlement) and the uncertainty of legal action by either party. But it is always a major cost to tax revenue.

A Position Paper is, then, fundamentally, an invitation from the ATO to open negotiations with the multinational taxpayer. Any debt to the ATO, including interest and late-payment penalties, is nearly always watered down in the interests of settlement. Government ministers are always happy to get their hands on the settlement money (which may be hundreds of millions of dollars), but the process is in danger of becoming a tactic for multinationals to pay only half or less of what was assessed.

In the case of tax *evasion*, the assets of the evader (often including his or her home) are seized. This has yet to happen in commercial tax disputes, although some prominent business identities have been handed long jail sentences.

The tax officers conducting the negotiations may not be entirely happy that large amounts of tax revenue seem to be repeatedly slipping from their grasp, but they will generally negotiate, because to do so is part of national policy commitments to the OECD for correlative relief. They represent their national interests to the extent that they can. It can take years, after the audit and negotiations with the company have ended, for an agreement to be reached,

A central problem is that a team of tax officers may spend years in audits of a single case before a settlement is made, and along the way the personnel (auditors and other staff) assigned to the case may change completely. It can happen that, if a major audit lasts more than 10 years, senior personnel may reach retirement age. In these situations there occurs a great leakage of knowledge and experience, which often results in a duplication of man-months of work for the ATO to regain the case knowledge that was lost.

Moreover, any settlement will require the agreement of the tax authority in the exporting country, as there will be an adjustment downwards of the taxpayer's income, and consequential correlative relief. And that will mean a partial refund of tax from the tax authority in the exporting country to the multinational because of what has retrospectively become an overpayment of tax due to the adjustment of the taxable value of income in the importing country.

The OECD has tried to resolve this issue by asking each of its member countries to appoint people with substantial international tax experience to negotiate on behalf of the multinational's exporting country with the tax authorities in the importing country where the audit and subsequent assessment has occurred.

The laudable goal is to eliminate the possibility of a company paying tax twice on the same income.

The process of correlative relief can also last for years. This is the foundation for the general view that transfer pricing basically results in the treasury of one nation robbing the treasury of another. That, however, is a simplistic view.

Arguably, the process involved in obtaining correlative relief causes a major delay for large companies that want to move on after an audit. But late-payment fees at rates of more than 10 per cent (or as much as 15 per cent) may be a sufficient reason for a company to show patience, allowing its home-country authority to negotiate the ultimate outcome for as long as it likes, particularly when the country's tax interests are also at stake.

The major impact of correlative relief is that it allows the multinational to use the tax authorities of its home country as an ally to further bargain down the settlement amount of taxes and penalties. The second benefit is that it receives some tax refund from the tax authorities in the country from where the goods were manufactured and sold to a subsidiary at an initially inflated transfer price.

Having said all that, however, completed audits involving correlative relief have, to some extent, been sidelined by the widespread use of tax havens and the use of entities that have no permanent establishment in any country. There is no overseas tax authority to deal with, and so there is no chance of the tax avoider getting any money back.

Audits consume enormous amounts of senior tax officers' operational review time — years, in fact. To some degree, it is a war of attrition between the multinationals and the ATO. Often there are frivolous issues, such as demands for the ATO to release confidential information supplied by other taxpayers operating in the relevant industry or market that, if agreed to, would make the tax officers subject to charges under the Crimes Act.

As the first transfer-pricing partner at Deloitte and Ernst & Young, I watched this happen time and again, and thought how wrong it was to charge fees of hundreds of dollars an hour (even in the late 1980s and early 1990s) in a dispute in which the partner corresponding with the ATO was obviously wrong in principle, law, commerce, and ethics. But it generated fees for the accounting firm. A delay in finalisation was worth money to the client if there was no interest charge, or if a discounted amount was agreed to upon finalisation.

The only possible justification for these delays in audit resolution was the huge amount of money at stake — in additional tax payments for past years, late-payment penalties, penalties in general, and additional tax in the future. As negotiations dragged on, these costs were always negotiated down to a great degree. Meanwhile, the overseas tax authority concerned (that is, in the country from which the goods or services had been exported, and which had already received at least some tax payments) stayed out of the decade-long audit. Its view was that any settlement was simply a raid on its national treasury, and it was disposed to act in its own national interest. It would take a few more years to think about it and haggle for a lower amount. This was possible, as no specific time limit was set for completion.

The damage caused to the global economy by transfer pricing is worse, longer lasting, and much more prevalent than that caused by the GFC. This may sound like an alarming claim, but it is true. How can a local business compete if it has no economies of scale, and pays tax while its multinational affiliate competitor does not? How long can it survive?

In Australia, the authorities and the parliament have lately bestirred themselves to do something about the elephant in the room. The *Tax Laws Amendment (Combating Multinational Tax Avoidance) Act* was passed in 2015, and came into effect on 1 January 2016. The legislation is apparently aimed at 'large multinationals [who] are suspected of diverting profits using artificial structures to avoid a taxable presence in Australia'.

A simple course of action, you might think. However, it cannot be unilaterally imposed, as it threatens the foundations of the OECD. The OECD's central rule is that a country which doesn't follow the policies of the OECD must leave the organisation — and the accounting concept of a permanent establishment is an OECD principle, which can only be changed with the agreement of all member countries. The 30 companies currently avoid tax by not having a taxable presence in Australia. It's hard to see how they could be penalised until and unless the permanent-establishment principle is amended by the OECD.

If the ATO is able to use the Tax Laws Amendment Act to stop, for tax purposes, global entities from acting as accounting-consolidated groups, this would have a devastating impact on their use of regional offices in Singapore, Hong, Kong, and other low-tax regions. If the ATO is unable to do so, it will be left ruing the current situation — whereby it won't be able to exercise Australian law when the entities involved are resident in other countries and by definition are not subject to Australian law.

Most recently, the Australian government has announced a new diverted-profits tax, which came into effect on 1 July 2017, targeting businesses that shift profits overseas through arrangements that result in less than 80 per cent tax being paid than would otherwise have been paid in Australia. A 40 per cent tax rate will be imposed on such profits, and is expected to raise the relatively minor sum of $200 million over the first four years — through the recruitment of an additional 1,300 ATO staff. Something about this maths doesn't add up.

This tax is modelled on the so-called Google Tax introduced in the UK in 2015, which is set at 25 per cent of taxable diverted profits, and is expected to raise about £350 million annually by 2017–18. One instant result of this new tax was Amazon's announcement in May 2015 that it would start paying tax in the UK on its retail sales rather than booking those sales through Luxembourg. As a result, the group will not have to pay the diverted-profits tax.

Ultimately, as with Australia's Tax Laws Amendment Act, both versions of such a tax are laudable, but seem to be in conflict with the OECD's insistence on a permanent establishment being the basis for tax laws — and the US's self-interest, as the headquarters of and recipient of at least some tax income from so many errant multinationals. The OECD itself is aware of the problem, but a solution may prove more intractable than seems likely on the surface.

Part II
Multinational Domination

Introduction

Until the end of World War II in 1945, Australia's exports were limited to gold and wool. In fact, since the mid-nineteenth century Australia had relied upon a single textile product that was shipped in hessian bales in its greasy condition exclusively to the UK's woollen mills. The rich squatters (sheep farmers) travelled to England annually to buy luxury goods and clothing. England was 'home', and every manufactured good was imported from there.

Gold was the other staple export. For decades, the price of gold was fixed globally by the United States at $US32 an ounce.

Several years after the end of World War I (in 1926, to be precise), the Australian government realised how isolated the nation would be if it were cut off from European (especially UK) manufactured goods. The solution was to establish a Tariff Board. This board set tariffs and quotas on imported goods with the aim of enabling local manufactured goods to be competitive. That is, the board set tariffs so high that importers were *not* competitive. British manufacturers were the only overseas source of supply. But they were twenty thousand kilometres away, and occupied with the European market.

Until after World War II the board did not do much except

impose prohibitive tariffs and quota restrictions; manufacturing activity remained minimal. The manufacturing exception (and he was exceptional) was Essington Lewis, the managing director of Broken Hill Proprietary (BHP) and Australia's director of supply during the war. Almost single-handedly, Lewis created a work culture that enabled BHP to monopolise the market for iron and steel to the point that imports were sought only if there was no quota available from BHP.

The history of the Tariff Board during the chairmanship of Godfrey Alfred (Alf) Rattigan and the prime ministership of Gough Whitlam marks the defining change in tariff policy from the end of the war in 1945 until 1990 through the tariff-review program.

Rattigan became chairman in 1963, and until 1972 the board continued its policy of giving manufacturers virtually whatever protection they asked for. Then, in that same year, Gough Whitlam became prime minister and cut tariffs by 25 per cent. But Rattigan headed a review of the manufacturing sector that was of even greater import than that tariff cut. As a result of Rattigan's review, for the next 25 years—with a brief tariff-reduction interruption under Liberal prime minister Malcolm Fraser—until the time of Paul Keating's ascendancy, first as treasurer and then as prime minister, tariffs and quotas maintained a downward trajectory. This downward movement on tariffs and quotas is the key to understanding how transfer pricing has had its ruinous effect on tax collections from multinational corporations.

In 1991, treasurer Keating famously announced in an early budget speech that tariffs were dead. With that, he also killed the textiles, clothing, and footwear industries. Together, these industries had employed over 400,000 people. Thus government, with the support of a compliant media and a rigidly 'free trade' doctrinaire attitude at the Productivity Commission (as the successor to the Tariff Board was then called), essentially gave space to the multinationals to devise a strategy to allow them to pay virtually no tax on profits resulting from sales made in Australia by their subsidiaries.

The subsidiary could operate forever (with bank support), underpinned by the commitment of the parent to meet the subsidiary's continually growing overdrafts. Some Australian multinational subsidiaries made losses every year for 30 years. If they halted manufacturing here and became merely importing distributors, they could use those accumulated losses as tax offsets, and not pay tax on the profits resulting from that role, either. This was the ultimate tax holiday.

This contention is very important, and the elements of its substantiation should be closely considered by anyone seeking to understand how and why multinational corporations came to adopt transfer pricing. The strategic unanimity between Keating and the economically correct chairmen and commissioners of the Productivity Commission resulted in the inevitable selection of fellow travellers as senior staff and commissioners. Keep in mind, too, that the commission historically had had the initiation and carriage of all industry-policy inquiries (through its predecessor organisations, including the Tariff Board) since 1926, even though inquiry references were drafted by Treasury.

The argument supporting this viewpoint is simple and historically verifiable. Essentially, when customs duties were high (that is, above the company tax rate) or when quotas were in place that restricted import volumes of consumer goods (such as cars, clothing, footwear, and cosmetics), multinationals could get no tax benefit from increasing the cross-border prices they charged to their subsidiaries. Had the multinationals increased prices to their subsidiaries under those circumstances, the consequential duty and sales-tax payments (until the introduction of the GST in 2001) would, in all likelihood, have reduced the after-tax profit of the parent company, rather than increase it. It would also have reduced the competitive position of multinational subsidiaries competing with local manufacturers.

Clearly, reducing combined duties and sales tax below the company tax rate gave room to multinationals to pocket the difference — to leave retail prices alone while increasing intermediate prices to their subsidiaries so that they constantly made losses. There were no 'passing on' provisions for those duty reductions, even though there had been for sales tax.

It is worth remembering the history of customs tariff and quota arrangements and their ultimate dismantling in order to understand that the Australian economy (manufacturing in particular) was destroyed by a flawed bureaucratic theory.

Although the demise of manufacturing was a direct consequence of government policy directed by a host of government and media ideologues, other developments played their role, too.

These included:

- The revolution in freight logistics from 1990 onwards;
- A major shift from sea to air freight following the introduction of air containers, with a consequential shortening of the supply chain;
- Australia's refusal (particularly under Paul Keating as prime minister) to use the internationally accepted and long-established dumping protocols of the World Trade Organisation;
- The advent of major information technology and quality management solutions to the manufacturing process

that enabled high-quality manufacturing at low costs in developing countries; and
- The absence of a major information-sharing arrangement between Customs and the Australian Tax Office.

A shorter supply chain and the rise of quality management and information systems that established China as the world's manufacturer were also obviously developments that no manufacturer focused on tax-free profits could resist. Australia was an early user and buyer of the products of the new regime, due to the disappearance of its manufacturing industry on account of the above developments and its proximity to China and other low-cost Asian manufacturing *entrepots*.

The failure of the Productivity Commission's predecessor bodies to include 'passing on' provisions in decisions to reduce tariffs was the final straw. The importers and their parent multinationals received a windfall gain when the tariffs were lowered. That hadn't happened when sales tax rates were reduced. In that earlier case, there were specific provisions for passing the benefits on to consumers. This major omission in commission recommendations was never questioned, either by the departments making cabinet recommendations following the inquiries, or by the media. The outcome was left to the market, as though it was operating freely. This produced a multimillion-dollar gain for car importers, for example. Consumers should have received at least part of the windfall benefit through price reductions.

The nexus between company tax and customs duties is an integral determinant of the transfer-pricing strategies of multinationals operating in Australia. When customs duties fell to 3 per cent, multinational suppliers were enabled to increase prices to their marketing and distribution subsidiaries to an extent that eliminated the latter's profitability and enabled them to avoid paying company tax.

Thus two courses of action were encouraged: the withdrawal of multinational manufacturing from Australia, and the sale of other substantial marketers and brand owners to multinationals. Meanwhile the Productivity Commission and senior public servants remained indifferent to 'passing on' provisions; and Treasury (through its responsibility for the major policies of the ATO) allowed losses to migratory companies involved in base erosion and profit shifting.

CHAPTER SIX

Shearers and diggers, 1890 to 1990

Until 1945, Australia was a sheep-farming and mining economy. Immediately after World War II, Australia still imported virtually all the manufactured goods it needed. Even those who made things were often imported, too, as our immigrant history attests.

Yet the Australian market wasn't completely open for imports until after 1960, when virtually all import quotas ended. But duty rates remained very high. With wool selling at a pound a pound until 1953, when the Korean War ended, some people (particularly sheep farmers) had plenty of money. They lived 'on the sheep's back'.

The average Australian worker's wage in the 1950s was about $10 (£5) a week. Western Australia and South Australia had small populations, and generally felt ignored by Melbourne and Sydney. During the Great Depression of the 1930s, Western Australia considered seceding from the Commonwealth. It was the only state trading with a budget surplus, and did not have to borrow money from the United Kingdom. England was regarded as the Mother Country. The wealthy graziers in the western districts of Victoria still regarded England as home, and often spent half their lives there. They could afford to. Most migrants came from England, Ireland, and Scotland before 1939.

In 1946, sea freight was limited to what could be carried by a wharf labourer to the ship's hold or secured on deck. The only air cargo in the post-war 1940s was high-fashion clothes, hats, and shoes from the European couturiers, and food and alcohol delicacies (and Fortnum & Mason baskets) for the rich graziers. Only they could afford the air- or sea-freight costs or the goods. They travelled to London with their wives for a few months every year, and bought fashionable clothing and hats to pack into their Louis Vuitton trunks.

The sea-logistics industry was still 25 years away from the advent of cargo containerisation. There were a few simple, small cranes at the major ports of Sydney and Melbourne. Newcastle and Port Kembla were bulk ports receiving iron ore and coal for the blast furnaces of BHP. The voyage to Europe by sea passed through the Suez Canal and took six weeks.

Most cargo was loaded by hand or trolleys. Wharf labourers stood in a pool of hopefuls every day at the port gates, hoping to be chosen by the tally clerks (whom they commonly had to bribe) to be given a day's work. The wharves were corrupt by common consent between virtually everybody concerned (Customs, water police, wharfies, and customs brokers), except the owners of the goods. Pillage was the name for goods broken open and stolen. Insurance company representatives met with Customs and the shipping company to determine whether the pillage had occurred at the Australian ports or at the overseas (usually UK or French) port. If the pillage had occurred in Australia, the high duty rate still had to be paid, even though the goods had disappeared.

Few international companies were operating in Australia, and most were in business selling manufactured goods or operating as manufacturers' agents. Most of these UK affiliates began production after World War II when the Australian government recognised that the country had no fundamental manufacturing base (other than BHP and a few multinational manufacturers of chemicals, paints, and batteries, or small subsidiaries of UK companies).

Australia's isolation and the absence of any pre-war development left the nation vulnerable. And no development was possible during the war. The absence of any manufacturing capability hindered our ability to support ships, aircraft, and the supplies essential for the troops, especially in Borneo, Malaya, and New Guinea. Most of our minuscule export trade in anything other than wool had been with the UK; but the German submarines had blockaded the UK.

Then, for 30 years after the war, Australia's defence needs were a powerful argument for high tariffs.

In those years, Australia had prolific, global-scale gold producers, particularly at Kalgoorlie and Coolgardie, but they were in the same risk category (as far as the UK was concerned) as South African goldmines. The UK was used to gold producers in remote colonies. Some of them produced nothing but promises and losses. Economies of scale had not been considered, and the price of gold had been fixed for decades by the Americans at US$32 an ounce.

Customs had no link with the Tax Office, other than the fact that most officers in both departments were Catholics. Until the 1970s, the religious tribe you belonged to was very important if you wanted a public service job. The Protestants went to the Post Office and Trade. Customs' potential recruits were asked by the personnel inspector where they went to school. Women were expected to leave if they got married.

Things had begun to change in the late 1940s and early 1950s, before the Korean War. Arthur Calwell, the minister for immigration in the last Labor government before Bob Menzies became Liberal prime minister, introduced an assisted-passage scheme (costing the migrant £10, or about the equivalent of two weeks' wages, for the six-week sea voyage from Europe to Australia) in the late 1940s. Many Southern European men (Italians, Greeks, and many other Europeans who had been in Nazi labour camps) could migrate to Australia if they committed to working on specific construction projects.

The Snowy Mountains Scheme and the Warragamba Dam were two of the major development projects built after the war. These were among the first infrastructure projects built in Australia since the Sydney Harbour Bridge had been financed by London banks (the debt for which wasn't extinguished until the 1980s). The migrants — men only — lived communally in huts away from the towns, which were often more than 20 kilometres from the site. They didn't go into town much. In those days, our shearers got to town from the sheep stations at least on the weekends.

Apart from gold and wool, Australia's export trade consisted of re-exported manufactured products to New Zealand that had come from the United Kingdom or the United States. No value was added — the goods were simply trans-shipped. They never left the port precinct, and didn't enter the Australian market for consumption.

The UK's decision to join the Common Market in 1973 was regarded as a betrayal of the parent-child link with Australia by many in the Commonwealth with historical and family connections to the Mother Country. Other national exporters, such as Japan and the US, began at the same time to succeed in selling their products in Australia in competition against the UK.

The twentieth-century response by Australian customs and tax authorities to the growth of international trade in goods was to tax imported and exported tangible goods and the profits of companies that engaged in the trade. We had duty rates that were among the highest in the world.

From the end of World War I, Australia's prevailing cross-border trade policy was to protect local industry. Australia's isolation from the rest of the world became very obvious in both world wars. The Tariff Board was completely protectionist, and said so. The government's aim was to enable the creation of a manufacturing industry, and the tool to achieve that aim was tariffs that were commonly at 45 per cent or even higher. In the 1980s, Australian carmakers held over 90 per cent of the local market, thanks to a combination of duty of 57.5 per cent and quotas (which were sold on the open market at prices as high as $2,000 per unit). Similar quotas and high duties applied in the textiles, clothing, and footwear industries.

The Australian customs environment

By 1960, when import licensing ended for all imports, except unwrought aluminium and shirts (unbelievably enough), the major forms of both international-border industry protection and revenue were a panoply of percentage (*ad valorem*) duty rates; fixed rates; a combination of fixed and *ad valorem* rates; sliding-scale rates; specific rates based on weight, quantity, or liquid volumes; and quotas. An entirely different tariff existed for alcoholic beverages, petroleum products, and excisable goods.

Many of these rates had been in place since the end of the war, but were irrelevant because of quantitative restrictions. For example, timber was dutiable at a rate of so many cents (or pounds, shillings, and pence) per 100 super feet.

My first consultancy job after leaving the Industries Assistance Commission (the name the Tariff Board took in 1972) was representing the Australian Timber Importers Federation to an IAC inquiry in 1979. I argued that the share of imports of softwoods in the Australian timber market from 1946 to 1978 had not varied from 20 per cent of the Australian timber building market, despite the fact that the percentage equivalent of a shilling per hundred super feet had changed from 40 per cent to 20 per cent. Duty had had no impact on Australia's timber requirements for Douglas fir and Asian timbers such as meranti, which were botanically hardwoods but could be worked as softwoods.

At least in those times, duty was not about revenue. It was about helping local producers. There were 2,000 timber mills in Australia (then represented by the Australian Timber Producers Council), but common sense won out. There was no point, from a protection point of view, in taxing softwood imports from Malaysia.

In retrospect, the entire post-World War II customs border-control process, with its complex systems and rules, probably added very little of value to the Australian economy. Yet we are still using the same process of individual customs entries that we had in the 1950s, even if the same goods are imported by the same importer 50 times a day. Millions of such customs entries are lodged every year.

Australia's tariffs were high, and some goods were subject to quotas. No attention was paid to taxing intangibles or profits earned in situations where there was no physical presence or permanent establishment in the market. Yet importer/traders and others who were involved in the transport of goods were taxed by the governments of the exporting companies.

CHAPTER SEVEN

The containerisation revolution

A huge change to logistics began in about 1967 when standardised 20-foot- and 40-foot-long steel containers for sea freight were introduced. These were fitted with locking pins that stabilised the containers when they were stacked on deck for sea carriage. Thus was revolutionised the process that had operated for hundreds of years wherein wharf labourers physically carried boxes or pushed carts, and handled small cranes to place cargo in the hold or remove cargo from the wharves.

Virtually all bulk commodities and manufactured goods were transported by sea at that time. Wheat and wool went in bags. Air freight had had only an insignificant share of international cargo movements (except for high-value perishable goods, jewellery components, and medical equipment) until the very late 1990s. Then the introduction of small, standardised air freight containers designed to fit precisely into the hold of an aircraft represented another major advance that again reduced handling costs and maximised space efficiency.

The development of the small air freight container and its quick adoption by the market immediately led to a rise in imports of high-quality components and equipment that were supply-chain time sensitive (and were no longer manufactured in Australia), and resulted in air freight gaining a larger share of the customs-clearance function (measured by the number of customs entries) than sea freight.

Many Australian companies that used to be manufacturers have since become assemblers of components, and providers of service and repairs to the after-market. The speed of supply and the availability of after-sales services provide their core market advantages. These have been enhanced considerably by the containerisation revolution.

Sea-freight charges for containerised cargo are less than 20 per cent of loose-cargo charges (other than for bulk commodities such as wheat and coal). Virtually all 'less than container load' (LCL) freight is containerised by shipping companies or freight forwarders, and exporters with less than a container load may pay up to seven times the container rate for this consolidation and subsequent deconsolidation. There is no cargo on deck other than containerised cargo, unless it unsuitable to go into the hold because of its size, shape, or weight.

(A hidden downside of the rise and rise of sea containers for international sea freight is that over the years since the 1960s, thousands of containers have fallen overboard in rough seas and are still floating just beneath the surface of the water in the major sea roads. They are a major hazard to all traffic.)

Non-container freight systems are still used for bulk cargo such as fuel, minerals, cereals, and other basic commodities that are poured directly into a ship's hold.

The physical change from the manual handling of freight to the movement of standardised containers by large overhead cranes has hugely reduced transport times and port costs. It has also annihilated the daily employment of wharf labourers.

Containerisation has generally and substantially reduced the length of the international supply chain. It has enabled 24-hour, seven-day-a-week direct delivery to the distribution centres of major customers such as Woolworths and Coles. Companies such as these operate their own dedicated truck fleets, and often visit individual supermarkets several times a day.

Side- and back-loaders have made truck drivers independent of client warehouse staff hours and available forklifts. They are able to drop off a container in the middle of the night or on a weekend at an importer's empty yard or warehouse premises. This efficiency has further concentrated the logistics task, and reduced costs and the number of days for international products to arrive into store. It has also converted the major eastern ports of Australia into 24/7 working ports.

That operational ability may have increased the prices that state governments realised when they sold the ports of Brisbane, Botany, and Newcastle. Port Melbourne, the largest container port, is now up for sale, too. Port sales have certainly helped New South Wales state finances enormously after what had been publicly exposed as decades of financial waste due to corruption. The total sales proceeds for Port Botany, Port Kembla, and Newcastle were about $6 billion.

By comparison, Macquarie Bank bought Sydney Airport in 2002 for $5.6 billion.

The containerisation revolution has allowed the establishment of 24/7 air freight hubs well away from towns and cities. Many of these are located in free-trade zones, where duty and VAT/GST are not payable until goods are removed from the zones. Goods may be stored for long periods (even years), further manufactured in the zone, and repaired and re-exported to neighbouring countries. The world has 3,000 free-trade zones in over 100 countries.

Australia (the Clever Country) has none. The lesson is obvious, but politicians on both sides of parliament have yet to learn it. Only the Northern Territory government and the coalition come up with a thought bubble supporting the idea from time to time.

Thirty years ago, I consulted to the Northern Territory government to establish a public bond supported by a customs-duty and refunds system guarantee underwritten by the NT government, but nothing came of it. Darwin is geographically close to Asia (particularly Indonesia), but has neither the substantial port infrastructure for shipping nor the quality of road networks required to connect it to Brisbane. Nor does John Howard's rail link from Adelaide to Darwin seem to have improved matters. Adelaide itself is a relatively small seaport that cannot compete with the major ports along the east coast.

In 2007, I also submitted evidence at an industry commission inquiry seeking a free-trade zone at Port Botany. The commissioner was David McBride, whom I knew well. He had been secretary of the Electrical Trades Union. David's conclusion was that a free-trade zone would disadvantage other Australian ports. Obviously, that was not the kind of conclusion reached in the hundred other countries that have them.

CHAPTER EIGHT

Unforeseen consequences

One of the critical factors contributing to the damage caused by transfer pricing in our economy is the growth in the efficiency of Australia's international trade in manufactured goods and services. Progress like this is not readily open to criticism. It is regarded as a social good.

However, there is a dangerous nexus between the huge growth of international trade in goods and services, and the extent and impact of transfer-pricing practices by overseas multinational corporations and their manufacturing affiliates. There is also an obvious nexus between the growth of imports of goods and services and the proportional decline in tax payments by multinational marketing affiliates.

The last of the Australian car manufacturers will soon be gone. Multinational affiliates will then supply all the goods and most of the services that are sold in Australia through their marketing affiliates. Many of the manufacturers' suppliers of components and after-sales products will also disappear. The car air-conditioning industry will disappear. Much of the car aftermarket is at risk.

Over 20 years ago, the Australian government of the day established a 'heads of agreement' between the customs and taxation departments, but nothing happened other than both departments being represented on some joint departmental committees. A Customs officer was on the transfer-pricing sub-committee at the Australian Tax Office, but I cannot remember him ever making a comment or asking a question.

It is fair to conclude that, in the past, neither the left hand of Customs nor the right hand of Tax had any knowledge of the processes and purposes of the other, nor of the company information and intelligence that each individually held.

An example will illustrate my meaning. About 20 years ago I was involved in a transfer-pricing project on behalf of the ATO in which the taxpayer had simply closed down its business premises and disappeared the day after a visit from the ATO. The tax officers didn't know where to look until they were told that Customs had exporter and importer address information for every customs entry. The taxpayer was a subsidiary of an Indonesian conglomerate, and had simply moved its office to Melbourne. It was quickly raided again, and ultimately paid large penalties.

A few countries (Canada, the United States, Ireland, and Holland) have merged their cross-border taxation operations. It is a good idea, but Australian Customs has been merged with the wrong department in a knee-jerk reaction to the 'Stop the Boats' issue. Customs border-control staff involved in halting the illegal movement of people into the country should have been split off and sent to Immigration. Border revenue should be part of an expanded ATO. The nexus between customs duty and tax is obvious for revenue policy; substantial synergies are available, and the two share strategic interests. Our international border management is still a dog's breakfast.

The only justification for Department of Immigration management would be if we shared a border with a poorer country and had to deal with the easy importation of drugs, as is the case between the US and Mexico. But on our remote, isolated island, our problems with drugs pale beside those along the US–Mexico border, and the activities of gangs in Mexico and other South American countries.

The present international focus on trade improvement demands an understanding of and an ability to combat the obtuse esoterica of the complex accounting strategies that the multinational corporations and their accounting advisers employ. Their only purpose is to avoid tax. There is no integrity or other functional purpose to the strategies.

Immigration, customs, and tax authorities should consider jointly developing a basic educational primer and hold seminars on transfer pricing for staff working in areas involving transfer pricing of international cargo and intellectual property cross-border movements. The present government and opposition need to explain how both political parties ignored the threat and then failed to counter the damage of transfer pricing to the tax base. Both sides of politics have formed governments in the period since 1990, but neither has tackled the cost to the Australian budget of transfer pricing. The ultimate loss to Australia's tax revenue is nothing less than disastrous.

In the past 30 years the common interest of the ATO and Customs in international trade policy, in so far as customs collects revenue for the government through duties and tariffs, has never been satisfactorily integrated into work processes or explained, either to the workers involved or to students at universities. Only a relatively few people have extensive experience and knowledge in both customs and taxation matters.

Rather, the knowledge across different departments has atrophied in this era of negligible duty rates. The valuation-calculation process is complex but, from a government perspective, its revenue outcome is eventually meaningless. For example, there is no longer a meaningful, public, annual publication of all imports by value, tariff classification, statistical code, and origin. It is almost certain that some statistical codes are being used incorrectly, but there is no scrutiny to ensure their accuracy. As duty rates have fallen, the knowledge provided by the Bureau of Statistics (ABS) has atrophied. Present ABS data is inadequate and difficult to examine publicly. Industry-source information is no longer available. The movement of Customs to Immigration will further degenerate in-house knowledge of customs classification theory and duty-calculation principles and practice. Most of the knowledge is in the heads of people of retirement age.

The revenue collected under the customs-valuation principles is small compared with tax collections for items that attract the taxes levied on alcohol, tobacco, and fuel. Those are taxed as specific rates (that is, based on the quantity of alcohol, tobacco, and fuel), and do not rely on the customs-valuation principles.

The trouble with the commission and its predecessors (and, for that matter, with Treasury) is that their view is monolithic. But industry policies considered in isolation from their impact upon other policies are usually doomed to failure, or have unintended adverse consequences.

A consequence of the drive to zero tariffs has been a major increase in the number of unemployed people. Centrelink's budget for 2015 was $134 billion, or about 10 per cent of Australia's national income. Treasury has undertaken research on the ageing of the Australian population, and the figures by 2030 become frightening. Many health-care and pharmaceutical benefits will have to be reduced. At the same time, the number of older unemployed or arbitrarily retired people living by consuming their assets and savings will rise enormously.

But remember, as Paul Keating announced 25 years ago, 'tariffs are dead'. They might not be as dead in the rest of the world as they are here, but contemporary taxation thinking has moved well past them as a mechanism for tax collection or industry protection. The complex array of rates up until the 1990s deserves to be dead.

The system of quotas and licences that the Labor governments of the 1980s developed were a disaster. The quota-allocation policy and bidding systems developed for cars, textiles, clothing, and footwear, and television licences provided wonderful opportunities for very ordinary entrepreneurs to simply game the auctions and sell the licences or quotas at higher prices to the companies that needed them. They made a lot of money cynically, without adding any value, by exploiting a process that traded on economic innocence and did nothing for Australia.

Australia seems reluctant to use measures for the taxation of cross-border trade similar to those that the rest of the major world economies use. We seem to have the approach that New Zealand often has with Australia: we always want to do something differently.

The Productivity Commission was too single-minded in the matter. It did not think outside the square of assistance anomalies and the necessity for their reduction. It produced reports and discussion papers full of unintelligible analysis that most of the participants in inquiries did not understand. This does not mean the analysis was not brilliant. It was just beyond the understanding of anyone who was not an economist. I doubt whether anyone today except old commission staff would be able to calculate 'effective rates'. Most economists would not know what they are, let alone be able to calculate them.

A practical new tax

There is an argument that Australia could close the gap between low duty rates and the much higher company-tax rate that the Productivity Commission's relentless drive to zero tariffs has opened up by introducing other taxes, such as road taxes. It could thus follow European practices and collect revenue without encouraging the return of inefficient local manufacturers.

Australia should follow the taxation strategies of Europe as quickly as possible. Europe works on the basis of high road tolls and high value-added taxes. Australia must increase the GST, to 20 per cent plus, and build a lot more road-toll collection points. A toll every 30-or-so kilometres in Europe certainly generates a meaningful amount of revenue for governments (rather than for the privatised toll operators, as in Australia). The highway between Sydney and Melbourne is an essential revenue-collection base, and a good way to tax the multinationals whose products are being transported. At present, it is used relentlessly by freight carriers for the major retailers, without any toll being imposed — even to offset the direct damage they do to the roads.

America operates differently. State taxes are important. Most US multinationals do not pay tax, either, but they have a great deal of money in the hollow logs of their subsidiaries' debtor ledgers and in tax havens, which can be produced if need be. It really is America Incorporated, though the partners keep an eye on each other. All multinationals in the US have a permanent Internal Revenue Service (IRS) officer resident within their headquarters. The rules about social relations with the multinational staff and Christmas gifts to the IRS staffers are draconian. They can go to jail if they take gifts.

What is blatantly obvious is that company tax is not working in Australia. The major companies involved are multinationals, and they are paying company tax at the first stage of the supply chain and avoiding tax on their ultimate revenue by incurring subsidiary losses that result in no company tax being payable on their real profits.

As we have seen, the reductions in customs duties over the 1980s and 1990s provided a powerful incentive for multinationals to increase the prices they charged their subsidiaries, which could not pass on the increases. The local companies lost money because they paid too much to their overseas affiliates. But that meant they did not pay tax. What was lost in one market (or many) simply ended up in the parent company's pocket somewhere else, where they did not have to pay tax or paid a risible amount.

Tax investigation officers have not used the connection that was established by a heads of agreement between the Australian Tax Office and Customs some 20 years ago. There has been no substantial attempt to create personal relationships among investigation officers from these two revenue authorities. There should be: Customs has important price and cost data and other information that can be provided to the ATO whenever tangible goods clear the customs barrier. For example, Australian customs-entry data can help the ATO to locate the importing affiliate and to understand the relationship between the import price from an overseas affiliate and the ultimate price in the marketplace. That price could then be compared with arm's-length market prices paid by importers that are not subsidiaries in Australia (if there are any).

Historically, tax officers can review how import prices have moved over time, and the extent to which parent or offshore affiliates have manipulated customs values in regard to duty reductions, currency movements, or competition from other multinationals. There is very little local competition to worry about. Customs maintains an historical record of all imports by a company over several years. The database can be downloaded easily, and costs just $100. I wonder how often ATO transfer-pricing teams access them?

The role of customs duty in the government's industry policy and revenue strategy is now extremely limited. Total customs duty collected in 2013 was about $5 billion. A substantial part of that total resulted from high duty rates for imported alcohol and tobacco products. In consequence, over the past 20 years there has been a substantial reduction in Customs' internal knowledge of the complex issues involved in the international valuation of goods transported across borders. Customs has never known how to value intangibles, even though the concept was part of its valuation process in the 1970s and 1980s (dealing, for example, with advertising and warranties).

Better communication, liaison, and exchange of information between the revenue authorities would benefit the ATO in particular. But the expansion of the border-control function in Customs has diverted its attention from the movement of goods and intellectual property. And the relocation of Customs to Immigration will further diminish the Customs-ATO partnership in relation to the classification and valuation of physical goods moving across borders and the subsequent management of the transfer-pricing practices of the global participants.

The best solution would have been to move the valuation and classification of imported goods to the ATO. Twenty-five years ago that was done with excise, in what turned out to be an efficient move that helped modernise excise tax collection. It had been inefficient and corrupt when Customs managed the excise function. Customs also collects GST on imported goods — a function that would be more sensibly carried out by the ATO.

Customs valuation principles and the arm's-length price

The concept of the 'arm's-length price' is central to both customs valuation and transfer-pricing analysis, but, as we have seen, the repositories of tax and customs' knowledge and experience of the concepts of classification and valuation often do not reside in the same government department and are not readily cross-referenced.

Customs valuation and the arm's-length price are fundamental twin concepts for determining the taxation levels of goods, intellectual property, and services moving across borders. The customs function is concentrated on tangible goods, but valuation often involves intangibles.

In some countries — such as Canada, Holland, and Ireland — taxes on goods and services (including GST, company taxes, and customs duties), and transfer-pricing issues and reviews have been made the responsibilities of a single revenue authority. This creates a single repository of knowledge, and ensures consistency of investigation and response.

These twin concepts were developed from drafting work completed after World War I in conjunction with the Treaty of Versailles. The Bretton Woods agreement (1945) was the outcome of a major meeting between Russia, the United Kingdom, and the United States. Their tax advisers were determined to ensure that global traders paid a fair share of tax or customs duties in every country in which they operated.

The rules are contained in the Brussels Tariff Nomenclature. The classification structure and classification principles for physical goods developed back then were brilliant, logical, and comprehensive, and are still in operation globally. The global customs tariff classifications begin with live animals, and progress through 99 chapters to antiques and works of art. Australia lacks only the thousandth tariff item: there are no Australian imports or exports of electricity.

The valuation is based on the open-market price for the sale of identical goods in an arm's-length sale to independent purchasers of the same quantity in the country of origin. This is known as the Brussels Definition of Value. This definition has not changed in the past 100 years, although the terminology has been modified for greater clarity at various times. These modifications allow for a number of valuation processes designed to meet the arm's-length standard, but do not depart from the basic Bretton Woods concepts.

Transfer pricing – the arm's-length principle

The principle for transfer pricing was developed by the OECD in a debate that lasted from the 1960s to 1989 among its member countries. There had been transfer-pricing cases in the early 1930s involving DuPont de Nemours and its Swiss dealings, but they had been isolated matters that did not stimulate taxation authorities to take any other initiatives. Australia was a participant in that debate, and, as a member of the OECD, had to accede to the agreed OECD transfer-pricing principles.

The OECD's purpose in establishing the arm's-length principle was to ensure that the multinational corporations of the world paid their fair share of tax in every country in which they maintained establishments. The principle allows for different cost and price additions for quantity, quality, scarcity, transport, payment delays, and costs of production. The reasoning is that the price determined in an arm's-length negotiation between buyers and sellers that are independent of each other is a price that can be used to determine objectively and fairly the taxable value of all international transactions for goods and services between buyers and sellers dealing across national borders.

The concept of independence was defined as the parties to the transaction having no ownership involvement with each other as parent and subsidiary, or as subsidiaries of the same parent company.

Opening the door to transfer pricing

Australian government-mandated tariff reductions in the past 25 years have been a fundamental causal factor in the rise and rise of transfer pricing by multinationals operating in and dominating the Australian market. It is critically important to understand that Australia's wholesale reduction in tariffs opened the door to transfer pricing. Yet no one seems to have reached this obvious conclusion.

Generally, the global push (especially from the United States) for so-called free trade has resulted in much lower taxes on imported goods. Australia has been a frontrunner in the race to establish zero tariffs. We are still negotiating free-trade agreements that simply are not agreements for free trade. At best they may be agreements for preferential trade.

What the Australian governments of the past 30 years have done is hand a multibillion-dollar gift to multinationals by eliminating the deterrent created by duty rates that were higher than company tax rates. The benefits created for multinationals made a mockery of whatever advantages Australia was supposedly to gain from the so-called opening of its economy.

Reducing customs duty levels in Australia was promoted as the way of creating an open, internationally competitive economy. Paul Keating's derogatory speech about our rusty-shed manufacturers at Redfern still resonates among the left-wing cognoscenti in Australia. Of course, we didn't create an open economy; instead, we allowed imports to enter, either duty free or at low single-figure rates, to cannibalise our local manufacturers. Import prices did not fall. The importers were not compelled by legislation to pass on the duty savings to consumers. It was a windfall gain for them. It was a lot of money that they never expected to receive and certainly didn't earn.

Manufacturing workers in Australia were demonised by the press as lazy and overpaid. It is embarrassing to remember the intelligentsia's push in the 1990s, led by the secretary of the Treasury, for a services-led economy. Then the emergence of China as the world's manufacturer destroyed any last hope of a substantial Australian manufacturing sector. The departing multinationals' manufacturing equipment was usually sold for a pittance or as scrap. The abandoned factories remained empty for 20 or more years until they were renovated as residential developments, or a use was found for them as storehouses and sales centres for imported clothing and footwear.

Paul Keating's rusty Redfern sheds are now either bulk-importing units or clothing and footwear wholesale outlets. None of what is sold at those outlets on busy retail Sundays is sourced from Australian manufacturers. Those rusty sheds used to employ Australians and a lot of migrants. Not anymore.

By eliminating tariffs and other barriers, and annihilating local manufacturing, Australia created a magnificent opportunity for multinationals to substantially increase the import prices of goods they manufactured overseas and marketed in Australia. Those price increases generally resulted in their marketing subsidiaries becoming chronically unprofitable. But that was part of the upside, as the parent companies were enabled to create manufacturing, marketing, and distribution entities that paid no tax at all. They had achieved the impossible tax dream. To this day, they either pay no duty (because there are no local manufacturers left to object to tariff concessions), or pay duty at a rate of 3 per cent. They pay less GST (or none) than in other countries. And they pay no tax on their profits, either by lodging in a tax haven or by manufacturing in a country that does not tax profits earned offshore.

Previously, through industry tariff rates, there was a legislated nexus between the price of the imported goods (the value for duty) and the amount of duty collected. However, free-trade agreements and a global appetite for lower duty rates have meant that very little duty is now collected. The major sources of revenue in most European countries are now VAT (our GST) and tolls on roads.

As duty rates have declined over the past 25 years, multinationals have increasingly focused less on minimising customs-duty payments and more on maximising the prices paid by affiliates in Australia to regional partners or parent companies. The higher the price of imported goods, the lower is the potential for subsidiaries to make a profit. In many cases, importing marketer distributers are incurring chronic losses. Some have done so for decades. But they are always armed with letters of comfort from their parents that assure the banks they will never default.

In an arm's-length environment, the Australian marketing and distribution affiliates that are always operating at a loss would be unable to continue in business. It is obvious that an arm's-length marketer-distributor repeatedly making such losses would have to close down. Its bank would not support it. Tax authorities pay insufficient attention to this certainty. They have taken the view that companies may be in loss for a few years after their establishment in a country, but they have seldom examined closely companies that have made losses for many years. It is well beyond time that they did so.

CHAPTER NINE

The multinationals' market strategy

International trade was much smaller and simpler in the first half of the twentieth century. Frenchman Louis Vuitton was still hand-crafting sea chests and leather luggage with lots of clever, strong compartments for those wealthy enough to afford his prices and the cost of travel on long sea voyages between London and New York. The vast majority of people never travelled more than 200 kilometres from home. A trip to London from the counties, or to Sydney from the Australian bush, was often literally the trip of a lifetime.

Import duties had been a key source of government revenues for centuries. The duty rates were high. Sources of supply were limited, and imports were often luxuries that could be purchased only by the wealthy when they travelled to other countries. Very few companies established manufacturing facilities in other countries. The parent company was the manufacturer.

Since then, mass production, efficiency of distribution, the establishment of global manufacturing hubs, the expansion of cities, the separation of manufacturing from marketing and intellectual-property ownership, and the burgeoning value of brand names and intellectual property have resulted in the consolidation of sources of supply into global companies. Such multinational corporations may have as many as 180 marketing and distribution affiliates and a handful of manufacturing plants located in low-cost production countries.

Multinationals are voracious acquirers of companies that fill market niches or that enable the reduction of competition in a market. They certainly own the great majority of global brand names and trademarks.

Other reasons for the concentration of world trade in relatively few hands have been the fundamental shift in the multinationals' international market strategy, and the shift from sea freight to air freight. Global brand names now dominate national retail markets, and are immensely valuable. Much of an enterprise's activity is focused on increasing the value of its brands globally.

Global brand names may be worth billions or tens of billions of dollars, and, as we have seen, the revenue accruing from their use usually goes to a subsidiary resident in a tax haven or a low-tax country that does not tax income earned outside the country. Estimates of the funds held in tax havens range between $US20 and $US30 trillion.

Such huge numbers often seem meaningless, so perhaps the best way of understanding their immensity is by comparing them to time measurements. A year is 365 days; a century is 36,500 days; a thousand years is 365,000 days; a billion years is a thousand times a million years; and a trillion is a thousand times a billion years. The annual income of the Australian economy is a bit over $1 trillion. So, the funds in tax havens are equal to the national income of around 30 Australias.

Improvements in sea freight and air freight times, and the subsequent cost reductions for movements of goods by air, have changed the international freight paradigm. Containerised sea cargo was introduced in about 1966, and massively reduced sea freight costs. The same evolution of specifically designed containers for transport by air is substantially changing the economics of international air freight.

What used to be called re-invoicing (that is, routing goods through several subsidiaries, increasing the in-house price, and adding no value but creating a tax benefit) is still prevalent. It is extremely difficult to determine whether charges by a regional office operating in a tax haven or free-trade zone or paying no tax for income earned for offshore management and back-office services represents an arm's-length and reasonable price for those services. Who can judge what the appropriate fee should be?

The free market's demise

The first difficulty in making comparisons between trade in the past and now is that world demand and supply have changed enormously in the past 30 years. Technology and communications via the internet have annihilated the methods of communication, sale of imported and exported goods, and government border controls that existed for over one thousand years. Global cross-border transactions can now be completed in a millisecond (rather than weeks or months), in circumstances where there is no physical evidence that international transactions have been completed at all.

There is no longer a direct nexus between the price charged for goods and services and what a purchaser would be prepared to pay in an open domestic market where there are direct substitutes available from other suppliers, and where consumers are aware of that opportunity. That is an obsolete concept, and no longer a general economic principle. There is no perfect knowledge in the marketplace, and consumers do not always act rationally.

Markets have hollowed out, and the number of suppliers to an individual market has diminished greatly. The market often takes whatever it can get from a single supplier or a few suppliers. It does not dominate suppliers and dictate the range of supply.

Even where there are more than a few suppliers, there is little true price competition. Add to that the fact that prying information from tax havens is next to impossible. It has been estimated that 83 of the 100 largest US corporations have dealings with tax havens that reveal nothing to any government department seeking information regarding the funds held in the havens. Consequently, tax authorities in countries that are major markets for global products have no opportunity to undertake the audits that might enable the full collection of taxes and penalties. The reason is the excessive amount of time it takes to discover the nature and purpose of transactions that are not readily disclosed.

Moreover, the near-impossible art of multinational interrogation by tax authorities is to know what questions to ask the Big Four advisers and to be able to understand complex replies. Audits may last for 10 to 15 years, and always result in a compromise that is almost felt as a revenue gift from the multinational involved.

From a market perspective, the reality is that competition for the consumer dollar has been annihilated. If there is no competition, there is no price competition. That certainty of market share or dominance is good for the multinationals, but not good for the consumer. We hear a lot about the operation of the free market, but it is simply government and multinational propaganda. The consumer is no longer king, and competition exists only in isolated market pockets. Multinationals do not care about price issues for individual consumers. They care about what their multinational competitor strategy is achieving in their market. And their most important concern is the market strength and popularity of their brand names.

In most product areas there are now no alternatives to the multinationals' goods. Small manufacturers have been bought out or have died out. The heirs of the founders of a business often lack the emotional commitment to its continuation, or may even feel antagonistic about the way the business consumed their parents; alternatively, there may be several heirs, among whom some may feel the commitment, but a business cannot be split into splinters. As a result, a family often sells a business when the founders retire or die. Taking the money is the easiest option. Even with a committed heir in charge, such family businesses cannot compete against the low-cost manufacture of products overseas, or against the deep pockets and tax-avoidance strategies of the multinationals.

These little companies don't employ the Big Four accountants. The Big Four sloughed off their middle-market clients 25 years ago with hourly rates the minnows couldn't afford.

The problems created by so few giant companies dominating such a large share of the global trade in goods and services begin with the fact that they don't generally pay their fair share of tax. The name for them — multinational — indicates their foundation philosophy. Their historical roots in any one country have atrophied, and mean little. There are exceptions, but these are often at the whim of a strong, entrenched chairman or chief executive. Those situations are, by their nature, temporary.

CHAPTER TEN

Transfer-pricing strategies

There is a major difference in both theory and practice between tax *avoidance* and tax *evasion*. Avoidance using the provisions of income-tax legislation is legal. Evasion is not. Tax authorities all over the world try (and succeed in some cases) to jail and confiscate the assets of people who *evade* taxes.

In Australia, a taskforce (Operation Wickenby, managed from within the Australian Tax Office) has the responsibility for finding and prosecuting significant tax evaders and, in some cases, has succeeded in sending the guilty parties to jail. Deputy Commissioner Mark Konza is now leading a large ATO taskforce that is conducting more than a 170 multinational audits specifically concerning the BEPS transfer-pricing issue in 2014–16. Those audits are likely to continue for years to come.

Transfer pricing comes under the heading of tax avoidance rather than evasion. The ATO does not confiscate money and assets in these cases. The perpetrators don't end up in criminal courts, and no one gets sent to jail with long sentences.

Apple and Google employ different strategies to avoid paying company tax and tax on profits in Australia. Both companies have been the subject of intense examination by the ATO. However, the basic foundation of their strategies are different.

Apple's total revenue in Australia in 2014, 2015, and 2016 was about $23 billion. Most of the revenue for sales was booked offshore, especially in Singapore. That country does not tax income earned in other countries. The income earned in Australia resulted in tax payments in Australia of $80.4 million in 2014 and $85 million in 2016. A billion is a thousand million, so about $80 million is about 3 per cent of $23,000 million. That is obviously only a fraction of the company tax rate in Australia. It's also just a fraction of the average Australian worker's tax rate.

The Australian Senate Inquiry into Corporate Tax Avoidance that reported in 2015 revealed a similar gap between those who were paying around 30 per cent in tax and those who paid tax at that rate with the zero missing. Most of the former had participated in advanced-pricing agreements with the ATO, and those that hadn't were enjoying a major tax-driven market advantage resulting from their failure to pay what most believed was a fair share of tax. Fairness is seldom created by working a tax dodge that your competitors don't use. Some of the company witnesses seemed to think they were doing something smart.

The Google strategy is based upon a global tax philosophy that is as outmoded now as the horse and cart. This concept is that a company without a permanent establishment in a country has no obligation to pay tax in that country. The wildfire growth of internet shopping in the world has delivered the 'no permanent establishment' principle a global reach. Companies without permanent establishments have no obligation to pay tax in any jurisdiction. The original tax lawmakers certainly never envisaged the internet and its massive impact on national retailers.

Internet imports now approach 20 per cent of transportable goods, most of which are retail products.

The 'permanent establishment' rule should go. Google would be devastated, but so were the carmakers, the textiles and clothing industry, and Australian workers generally when customs policies were gradually cut. If change is inexorable, then outdated tax tricks should also be eliminated when they are past their use-by date.

Four examples of haven uses

1. Google's six-step strategy:

Step 1: Google pays a major fee to an intellectual-property licensee company in Ireland for advertising costs in Europe (which may or may not have been incurred). That fee is taxable at 12.5 per cent.

Step 2: The Irish licensee company buys the intellectual-property licence from a Netherlands licensor company that collects a royalty payment for the intellectual property.

Step 3: The Irish licensee company gets a tax deduction.

Step 4: Another entity in the Netherlands is taxable on the royalty payment.

Step 5: The Netherlands company pays a royalty (an accounting deduction), is not a tax resident of Ireland, and has no interest in the Irish holding company.

Step 6: The Irish company is managed in Bermuda.

(The Irish government discontinued the so-called 'double Irish strategy' during the 2014 OECD initiative on transfer pricing.)

2. Amazon owns Amazon EU Sarl, which is a Luxembourg resident company.
   - Amazon sells to its subsidiary, Amazon UK, which has a Berkshire office.
   - Amazon also stocks books from UK publishers and distributors, which it sells direct to customers.

- Contracts and funds pass directly between Amazon EU Sarl and the customer.
- Amazon has no permanent establishment.

3. Apple's offshore distribution structure:
   - Apple Holding Company receives dividends from Apple Sales International Ireland.
   - That income comes from foreign-based company sales made by offshore distribution subsidiaries that receive income from customers.
   - The manufacturer is Chinese, and deals directly with Apple Sales International in Ireland.

(This strategy may also be terminated as a consequence of the change in the Irish government's policy.)

4. Starbucks is a US-based parent that uses royalty payments, internal loans, and goods pricing. It owns two Dutch subsidiaries that, in turn, are paid royalties by Swiss and Dutch companies.

Internet trading and the internet economy

Most multinationals have virtual shopfronts on the internet. That is certainly true for cosmetics, toiletries, and fragrances; textiles, clothing, and footwear; technology products; appliances; long-life foodstuffs; and virtually any product that can be delivered to the consumer's door.

Australia has had the highest duty-free and GST-free thresholds for internet imports in the world. The only exceptions have been alcohol and tobacco products, which remained dutiable at rates that range from 50 per cent (for beer), to a 100 per cent for spirits, to over 1,000 per cent for tobacco products if the calculation is based on the cost of production for cigarettes. Those goods are also subject to higher duty rates in virtually all countries. The excise-equivalent duty rates on those products obviously provide a lot of government revenue, and internet importers would certainly start businesses importing those goods if there were a major duty or excise differential. The lower rates would also drive local producers out of business.

Internet trading represents about 10 per cent of total retail sales of non-perishable goods in Australia. The internet's market share of the retail industry is rapidly increasing, and constitutes a major threat to the profitability and, ultimately, the viability of Myer, David Jones, Harvey Norman, and other retail chains that employ hundreds of thousands of (mostly young) Australians.

Many people go to the major shopping centres solely to get information about clothing and footwear sizes and colours, and to test cosmetics, toiletries, and fragrances. The major retailers are knowingly participating in their own demise by providing this service, but have little choice if they want to avoid antagonising potential customers. But these people then go home and buy the products online from overseas retailers. Delivery costs to the purchaser's door are relatively low, and door-to-door deliveries are dominated by Australia Post and German company DHL.

Customs was a long-time stout proponent of the Australian customs duty-free threshold of $1,000. It argued that lower values would make the customs valuation and classification task more onerous, and that the amount of duty collected would not justify the additional examination costs. That position was even supported by the Productivity Commissison, as recently as 2011. Yet the task was no barrier for other nations affected by the internet trade. Europe has thresholds of less than €50 ($A80), and the United Kingdom's is about £20 ($A40).

Customs has at least had a general bylaw for the past 40 years that provides for passenger concessions when overseas travellers return with not-for-resale items bought on their trip. A Passenger's Card has to be completed by all incoming passengers, and duty is collected at the arrival terminal at the ports. But there is considerable pressure on Customs to process arrivals quickly, and the duty-collection process is haphazard; it does, however, theoretically involve standard international tariff classification and valuation procedures. Only a few officers are available at the main airports to assess dutiable imports possessed by thousands of arriving passengers. Import shipments (whether by air or sea) and passengers present a variety of risks as potential sources of drugs, weapons, or other prohibited imports. The number of border-control staff needed to tackle these tasks has grown since the explosion of internet imports and the general reduction in duty rates.

There have always been criminals dealing in imported goods and the drugs market, but the explosion of air freight shipments arising from internet-sourced imports makes the customs task more difficult. This is not a problem exclusive to Australia, although Australia's uniquely generous duty threshold tends to encourage a lax border-control process that increases the ease of imports of drugs and other prohibited substances and products (such as firearms, flick knives, and explosive devices).

Moreover, the classification, valuation, and tariff-concession tasks (and consequentially, in-house knowledge) of Customs have declined substantially as duty rates have fallen over the past 20 years. Customs' technical work in the areas of entry examination — including valuation, classification, rules of origin, and quarantine — has been hit greatly by technology and a shift to small containers for air freight.

The OECD has identified value-added tax as the tax most threatened by the ability of multinationals to trade on the internet, so it might have been expected that the growth of personal imports would have been a compelling reason for Australia to expand its examination of incoming goods, at least to the extent of using the systems employed generally throughout Europe and the United States, and apply its GST to them. But, no. Courtesy of both major political parties, a uniquely Australian policy of free-market internet largesse operated until, at five minutes to midnight, its proponents had to face reality.

CHAPTER ELEVEN

Transfer-pricing methodologies

When the OECD first selected the main ways of determining the arm's-length price, it had in mind that the methods be considered in a particular order when used for transfer-pricing analysis. The idea was to create an objective and common analytical basis that all multinational corporations could use to demonstrate that their cross-border transactions with affiliates met the arm's-length standard.

The OECD's preferred order of methodology was as follows:

The comparable uncontrolled price (CUP)

This method requires determining what would be the arm's-length price for a transaction between unrelated sellers and purchasers. Being at arm's length means that the seller or the buyer has no control over the other party that might allow it to influence the price or conditions of sale.

The transactional net margin method (TNMM)

In this method, a company is chosen from among thousands of companies precisely because its financial data gives an outcome that serves the interests of the multinational — that is, it delivers the lowest-tax outcome.

The resale-minus method

This involves beginning with the retail price and then deducting import costs, warehousing, and other local to-market costs to arrive at the remaining amount. This amount is then treated as the actual price between the affiliated companies, which may be the parent company or subsidiaries of the parent company, and the local company.

The cost-plus method

This method involves looking at the cost of the goods and adding all additional charges and expenses in bringing the goods to the point of sale to an arm's-length party.

In fact, the resale-minus and cost-plus methodologies are seldom used. The choice in the past 25 years has been between CUP and TNMM. Even then, virtually no multinational has used CUPs.

Objective analysts have always regarded CUPs as the best methodology. Yet, until recently, tax authorities have generally disregarded it in favour of the transactional net margin method (TNMM), as tax officers considered the precise comparability tests too onerous, and undertaking the research and analysis too comprehensive and expensive. Originally, the search for CUPs was expected to find goods or transaction charges that were exactly comparable in specifications, quality, volumes of sale, technology, and any other basis of comparison with an uncontrolled price. The judgement that CUPs is too burdensome and precise to be useful in practice by national taxation authorities has cost world economies hundreds of billions of dollars in tax-payment delays and excessive analyses that take many years to reach finality.

However, recent Federal Court decisions in Australia (Roche Pharmaceuticals and SNF Australia, which are discussed below) have eased the analytic strictness that the Australian Tax Office had considered necessary for the first method, which involved finding perfect CUPs.

The fact is that a slightly imperfect CUP is a lot more persuasive than a self-serving TNMM, in which one company is chosen from a huge number of companies precisely because its financial data gives a self-serving outcome.

In Australia, this self-serving choice of methodologies has been rejected in two major court cases. SNF Australia manufactures organic coagulants and synthetic flocculants. The tax commissioner took the SNF case to the Federal Court, which on appeal went to a full bench of the Federal Court. Both courts found that, essentially, the precision of CUPs did not have to meet the comparability standard considered necessary by the ATO or, for that matter, by the Big Four advisers to SNF. In 2010, the full bench appeal was lost unanimously: all eight judges ruled against the commissioner.

In Roche Pharmaceuticals, a single judge in the Victorian Court of Appeal reached the same conclusion. The tax commissioner did not appeal against the decision in favour of Roche Pharmaceuticals.

If anything, these decisions against the ATO in favour of a slightly relaxed and less onerous CUPs should, ironically, enable the ATO to insist more sturdily in the future on such a modified CUPs being used, as it in fact serves the tax office's purposes more than it does the purposes of the taxpaying multinational.

Indeed, these decisions have caused a great deal of uncertainty for companies involved in related transactions. Virtually all multinationals and affiliates (and the ATO) have relied upon the TNMM on the basis that applying the CUP was untenable. This was because there were always differences between the products and services — even if the differences were trivial, and they were for sale at comparable prices in the same markets — thus rendering the CUP requirements too precise to enable any comparison.

Again, it can be assumed that almost all transfer-pricing analysis in Australia over the past 25 years on behalf of multinationals has been undertaken by the Big Four. And it would be interesting to know what percentage of multinational transfer-pricing analysis has employed the TNMM. I think it would be over 90 per cent.

Comparables shopping for the TNMM

Twenty-five years ago, consultants seeking a ruling on sales tax would travel from tax office to tax office in Australia, shopping for a favourable decision. Once they got it, that was the decision they would use for their client. They did not disclose to the ATO that they had shopped around.

These days, a variation on that strategy has generally been used in transfer-pricing studies before they are submitted to the Australian Tax Office. International databases that often include thousands of companies of all shapes, sizes, and character are used when providing functional analysis to the ATO. The consultants provide no substantial justification for why any particular company is chosen and another rejected.

The TNMM has been so successful a methodology for the global minimisation of tax and the generation of fees by multinationals that it has displaced virtually all other methods. That includes those methodologies that the OECD initially regarded as the primary methods that had to be considered before using the TNMM.

Twenty-five years ago, the TNMM was regarded as a last resort in rare circumstances. It would be used in cases where the analyst concluded (and the tax officers agreed) that relevant data were not available for the application of the CUP, cost-plus, or resale-minus methodologies.

The simple reason for its popularity is that, from the perspective of the Big Four accounting firms, it is relatively easy to derive appropriate (if not self-serving) comparables. Equally simple (and self-serving) has been the view that comparables had to be perfectly comparable, thereby ruling out the CUP method. Yet literally thousands of potentially comparable balance sheets can be purchased from database sources for a few thousand dollars.

The relative simplicity of functional analysis using the TNMM has also enabled the Big Four to cope with the avalanche of work they have dealt with in the growth of transfer-pricing consultancies. They have persuaded many tax officers carrying out transfer-pricing audits that it is the only practical methodology.

It would be valuable to discover whether the Big Four have ever concluded that some multinationals didn't meet the arm's-length standard for some products or intellectual property in particular markets, and that prices to their affiliates had to be reduced. In a PwC submission to the OECD, Brussels partner Isabel Verlinden (the leading transfer-pricing partner in Europe) pointed out that 'policies should be coherent, consistent, reasonable and economically credible'. That sounds excellent, but is it always true and always presented objectively by the Big Four?

The credibility issue would often create some interesting discussions between the auditors and the transfer-pricing partners. I was once in that position, and was told by the audit partner that my concern about a company's transfer-pricing documentation and analysis was immaterial. That was obviously a great way of avoiding an audit issue that the company management would not have liked. It was not a credible response, but it was the end of the discussion. Twenty years ago, the audit group ruled the firm because it generated most of the recurring fees. An adjustment of millions of dollars wasn't considered material! The company under consideration wasn't a global giant in Australia, but was a big name in the world market.

A multinational client doesn't expect its accountants to tell it that it isn't paying enough tax, especially when the Big Four firm doing the audit also audits all the global affiliates of the multinational. Being given an unpleasant analysis by an audit manager will not change the auditor, but it might change the audit manager.

Ultimately, this strategy must come to grief, as it has in both of Australia's transfer-pricing court cases. It came under the spotlight during the latest major examination of base erosion and profit shifting (BEPS) initiated by the OECD. How much will it have cost in revenue and time for the nations of the world before BEPS is finally consigned to the dustbin of history?

As was noted earlier, in the appeal by the tax commissioner against the SNF decision, a Full Federal Court bench of eight judges unanimously concluded that the ATO's strict interpretation of CUPs was impractical, and meant that taxpayers would never be able to employ this method because of the rigid comparability standards being applied.

Until the late 1990s, the ATO had about 20 major regional tax offices (with as many as 1,000 members of staff in each one) scattered around Australia. To some extent, they were individually able to give binding rulings that were not consolidated or reviewed by a central office. This resulted in the decision-shopping referred to above, where consultants unhappy with one tax-office decision would simply go to another office to obtain a friendlier outcome for their clients.

Until Australia's two recent transfer-pricing court decisions were finalised, this process was all there was. The Roche Pharmaceuticals and SNF Australia cases have changed that situation, but more court cases are needed. There needs to be a history with different courts and judges, as there is in the United Kingdom. That will create a continuing judicial dialogue — analysis, opinions, and precedents that range across various facts and circumstances. That body of knowledge and opinion needs to be examined and sifted by experienced legal intellects, and then applied to the varying circumstances and facts of different cases at different times.

However, these precedents were not part of the parliamentary debate over retrospectivity in the case of transfer-pricing abuse. That legislation passed both houses of parliament in September 2012 with the help of the independent senators and the Greens. As a consequence, the ATO can now revisit tax cases back to 2004, even if the audits have been closed.

The present Chevron case in the Federal Court is on foot as a consequence of the retrospective transfer-pricing legislation.

Chevron Asiatic Limited contributes the first three letters of the Caltex name. The Tex is Texaco. These enterprises are two of the largest oil and gas companies in the world. In the first instance, Chevron looks to have lost the case. The only problem with the case is that it will take a long time to be finalised. Australia and Chevron almost cannot afford to wait for what might be six years before a final outcome is reached that cannot be further appealed. Many other transfer-pricing audit settlements made over the past 25 years are likely then to become subject to review on the grounds of the principle established in this case.

There is no intellectual or moral foundation for the behaviour of the multinationals. They are the robber barons of the twenty-first century. They do things because they can. They create tax-minimisation strategies because they can. The only way to make them accountable is to challenge their arrangements successfully through the legal system. The difficulty with that process is that it may take as long as seven years and cost millions of dollars for a major case. Losing the case is not an option for either side. The Chevron case will set a precedent if it gets as far as the High Court. The arguments most probably will revolve around the retrospectivity of the legislation, which is anathema for many practitioners and jurists.

Meanwhile, the damage caused to the global tax base and economies in general by self-interested transfer-pricing analyses and the use of tax havens will continue unabated.

Multinational shape-changers

For some years, the Australian Tax Office has been aware of the profit-shifting opportunities and strategies employed by multinationals when they deal with their own affiliates in overseas markets.

The relevant ATO Taxation Ruling 2011/1 is named, 'Income Tax: Application of the Transfer Pricing Provisions to Business Restructuring by Multinational Enterprises'. As is always the case with Australian taxation rulings, it is the ATO's view of the law. This ruling is, essentially, directed at base erosion, and is intended to counter profit shifting. It seems, though, that the ruling has not had much success as in deterring multinationals from using BEPS strategies.

Australian society has changed radically in the past 20 years. Millions of women are having children later, and returning to the workforce when their children are pre-school age. The ATO cannot create a ruling to halt the phenomenon of the temporary migration of young and clever working couples, often with small children, to low-tax countries such as Singapore and Hong Kong. What Tax Ruling 2011/1 does achieve is to explain clearly and cogently how multinationals restructure and move their functions, assets, and risks to other tax jurisdictions that impose lower tax rates or no tax at all. Singapore and Hong Kong are two very successful examples of economies that have attracted major multinational regional offices and other facilities because they do not tax income earned offshore.

More mundanely, in the past 40 years the production, marketing, and sales functions of multinationals have been stripped from what used to be a single manufacturing, intellectual-property developing, holding, and marketing company in a major market and divided among several functionally specialised business units in several countries.

The functional division is often as follows. The chain of global supply to the market begins with research and development, the creation of brand names, testing and quality control, materials' development, including packaging and components sourcing, and cost-management analysis. These processes used to be part of a linear development over several years in one or a few national locations (if the customs duties were high enough, and/or there were other non-tariff barriers in several countries).

Until after World War II, the head office (or head factory) was often in Europe or the United States. Then Japan and Korea became manufacturing powerhouses that supplied their own and other multinational products to the world. They have now been supplanted by Chinese manufacturers that have captured and dominated the world's manufacturing task. China now produces high-quality brand-name products, but does not own the manufacturing knowhow, the brand names, or the marketing and sales intellectual property. It is also still manufacturing low-cost, poor-quality goods; but that will end as quality-control philosophies penetrate the high-volume manufacturing functions. This shift occurred in Japan in the 1970s.

Manufacturing knowhow, and permission to use a brand name and any distinguishing logos, shapes, and colours, are provided by the owners of the brand names. They are also the owners of superb quality-control techniques. These have been embedded in Chinese manufacturing after a start-up period that was much shorter than Japan's experience from the 1950s.

The acquisition (or loan) of manufacturing-process intellectual property and global brand assets, combined with lax environmental standards, extremely long and efficient production runs, and low wages, have resulted in an almost complete transfer of the manufacturing of quality goods to China. China has also captured the world's textiles and clothing manufacturing task by creating very long production runs that cover the different seasons in each hemisphere. These global production runs have virtually annihilated even the New York export clothing industry.

In the past, multinationals established factories in smaller countries because of tariff or non-tariff barrier to imports. By the end of the twentieth century, these barriers had been largely dismantled or replaced with more subtle forms of non-tariff protection. The removal or reduction to meaninglessness of such barriers has been the cost-saving engine for BEPS. What is left are nuisance tariffs that do not affect decisions about local or imported sourcing.

When a multinational entered a market, it usually used arm's-length marketer-distributors. This strategy involved little capital expenditure and small losses if the new market initiative did not work. Agreements were normally for five years, and were construed and drafted, in the US case, in accordance with the law as it applied in the tax-haven state of Delaware. That gave the offshore marketer-distributor little chance of hanging on to the franchise if it wanted to.

In Australia, from the 1970s to the early 1990s, Japanese multinationals (especially motor vehicle, motor bike, and outboard motor makers) appointed Australian marketer-distributors in all states except Victoria and, occasionally, Queensland. In one of these states they established a subsidiary that was, effectively, the major distributor, which was led by Japanese managing directors who often stayed in Australia for the rest of their careers. Because they stayed so long, they lost their position in the Japanese salaryman management hierarchy, and their children no longer fitted into the Japanese school system. The major Australian subsidiary became the source of quality control and intellectual-property management, and also was a standard against which other state distributors were measured. At the end of the agreement, the Japanese parent company would buy the Australian distributor's business.

Few US parent companies followed the Japanese model. They simply ended the distribution agreement, based on the law in the state of Delaware after five years, when they believed that the Australian market was ready for a US-owned and -operated local subsidiary. Sometimes they paid something for the distribution/ sales knowledge to the distributor they had acquired, or made them an ambassador for the company for a few years.

Base erosion and profit shifting has supplanted that multinational strategy. It involves a fundamental shift in the functions, assets, and risks of the multinationals' affiliates that is specifically intended to shift profits to lower-tax locations.

Taxation Ruling 2011/1 discusses the tax issues and its view of changes 'involving the conversion of distributors to sales agencies and manufacturers to providers of manufacturing services', and the movement of major maintenance performance (as in the Qantas relocation of maintenance to Singapore).

A common process (probably now complete) has been the relocation of call centres to Asia, India, and the Philippines. They were often moved first from Australian cities to Australian country towns, where they were a great boon to country families. If the farm didn't provide a living, the women of the family often worked at the council, local call centre, or in retail stores in town during the week, and went home on the weekends. That community-friendly setup did not last long.

The relocation offshore isn't always customer friendly, but it saves costs, and the multinationals often have a stranglehold on the Australian market. They are the only supplier, or one of two.

The tax ruling doesn't just cover changes affecting the workforce. It deals with changes in the ownership of intangibles such as brand names, trademarks, and patents. These have values that are measurable. Other, unquantifiable intangibles that are often shifted offshore are related to manufacturing and sales techniques, quality control, and environmental issues. Commonly, key employees are kept on for a while to ensure that the transfer of marketing and manufacturing knowhow is complete.

In an arm's-length situation, the multinationals would have to write off losses contracted by their affiliates. As things are, they can keep these losses on their books and use them for years to offset profits that accrue at their affiliates because the marketing-distribution activity (combined with very low-cost offshore manufacturing and strong local brand names) is a wonderful profit source, particularly if no tax is paid.

Taxation Ruling 2011/1 also requires that the price paid by a parent to its subsidiary for movement offshore of the business activities of the subsidiary be at arm's length. It would be no easy thing, during the performance of an audit, to determine whether that had been done. Merely getting hold of the fundamental transaction information would be a lengthy process.

There is a flaw in the ATO ruling's procedure for determining the equivalent of an arm's-length transaction between a subsidiary and the parent office of a multinational company. Even in circumstances where there has been an independent distributor or marketer, subsidiaries do not have the bargaining power necessary to name their own terms when a multinational decides to terminate or vary an agreement. The negotiating power resides with the party that owns trademarks, brand names, manufacturing knowhow, and all the other elements that make up a successful product to the point that it dominates a market. The multinational also has the capacity to invest in and create new products that often build upon decades of research and development.

The almost foregone conclusion is that a local arm's-length marketer-distributor ending an agreement with a multinational supplier will have to be satisfied with what it can get. There has even been a philosophical contention between the northern and the southern hemispheres as to the value of assets held between manufacturers and brand-name owners and their arm's-length marketers around the world.

The North (Europe, the US, Japan, and Korea) comprises nations that have a long history of developing, investing in, and owning global products and services. The South includes Africa, South America, and parts of Asia and Oceania. Some countries in the South are becoming major manufacturers and exporters. They are also, increasingly, consumers of multinational products in their own retail markets. The North's argument is that they take the risk, provide the original finance, own the intellectual property, and create the brand name, the product range, and the marketing strategy. They are the creators of new products, and the owners of the chain of product development that often stretches back decades or longer. Eli Lilly, Union Carbide, and Louis Vuitton, for instance, began in the nineteenth century.

The final part of the debate is the argument that the South provides a large proportion of the consumers for multinational products and services. They create the marketing intellectual property at least in their own backyard, with its particular circumstances and market conditions. They know the market and the consumers. They are closest to the domestic supply chain, government requirements, and local conditions, and can often see the future for their products.

CHAPTER TWELVE

The OECD Action Plan, and the Big Four's responses

As the threat to the global economy from the toxic multinational practice of base erosion and profit shifting has become impossible to ignore, the OECD has finally sprung into action. In September 2014 it produced a 15-step Action Plan, and issued a brief (12 pages) explanatory statement in which it outlined seven actions (or steps) nominated for delivery in 2014. These were as follows:

- Action 1: Address the tax challenges of the digital economy.
- Action 2: Neutralise the effects of hybrid mismatch arrangements.
- Action 5: Counter harmful tax practices more effectively, taking into account transparency and substance.
- Action 6: Prevent treaty abuse.
- Action 8: Assure that transfer-pricing outcomes are in line with value creation: intangibles.
- Action 13: Re-examine transfer-pricing documentation.
- Action 15: Develop a multinational instrument.

The action-plan items nominated by the OECD for discussion and further action in 2015 (and possibly for years beyond) include:

- Action 3: Strengthen CFC (controlled foreign company) rules.
- Action 4: Limit base erosion via interest deductions and other financial payments.
- Action 7: Prevent the artificial avoidance of permanent-establishment status.
- Actions 9 & 10: Assure that transfer-pricing outcomes are in line with value creation for risks and capital, and other high-risk transactions.
- Action 11: Establish methodologies to collect and analyse data on BEPS and the actions to address it.
- Action 12: require taxpayers to disclose their aggressive tax-planning arrangements.
- Action 14: Make dispute-resolution mechanisms more effective.

The next generation of multinationals that will follow the path of the Apples, Googles, and Amazons is already in formation. Who will they pay tax to if they have no permanent establishment?

One leader of PwC's global transfer-pricing practice said in a monthly newsletter that the world was already a digital economy. That is an elitist and insular view which ignores virtually all the undeveloped countries and the emerging economies. It also ignores a lot of older and poorer citizens in modern economies (including the largest economies in the world) who are not computer literate and never will be. In Australia, the poor and the old line up every morning (spilling onto the street) at post offices to pay their utility and other essential bills by cash. They are not part of the internet economy. They don't own a computer. They can't afford to buy one or to pay monthly internet fees.

Achieving the OECD's BEPS action plan in a decade is going

to make Rumpelstiltskin's goal of spinning straw into gold seem like a kindergarten task. To get agreement from OECD members on the arm's-length standard took decades, from the 1970s to the 1990s. All agreements must be unanimous.

The action plan does not discuss the fact that the Big Four firms have already created thousand-page documents justifying their transfer-pricing policy, strategy, client activity, and initiatives. The plan is at pains to avoid directly criticising them.

An unforeseen result of the action plan is that it is effectively a strategic blueprint for the Big Four to make many more billions of dollars in fees from the multinationals that are threatened by the OECD initiative and the support given to it in Europe. The US members of the Big Four have been careful not to be aggressively negative, although a few politicians have expressed such views. Asia has been quiet on the subject.

It would be interesting to know what the global transfer-pricing staff numbers are in the Big Four today. The task has certainly swelled staff numbers and annual income figures in the past 25 years. Extrapolating from the UK parliamentary report (see Appendix F), the Big Four have earned about $500 billion in global fees from transfer-pricing consultancy in the past 25 years.

The problems will not derail the OECD action plan, but may delay or modify the outcome. There is simply too much money involved to expect that, ultimately, the multinationals will go quietly and start meeting their tax obligations. The huge iceberg of past obligations and audits in progress, and the complex role of correlative relief, won't just melt away. The multinationals are not alone on this issue. Where they have overpaid tax in other countries and underpaid it in export markets, the tax authorities in the exporting markets are not enthusiastic about refunding tax to their home multinationals. Japan, Germany, and Holland have certainly dragged their feet. Correlative relief always takes years.

The entire list of the OECD's 15-step action plan is provided below. I have indicated what each step entails, and have included some comments after each item to indicate what may cause delays and road blocks in the program.

1. Tackle the tax challenges of the digital economy

This requires dealing with companies that have a significant digital presence in a country without being subject to taxation because there is no nexus under current international rules.

Comment: The problem here will be how to create international sanctions that dissuade multinationals operating without permanent establishments in any country from continuing to exploit the present legislative vacuum to pay no tax or risible amounts of tax. Tax should not be a donation to the economy. If there are financial sanctions, why would the multinationals care? Any such sanctions would be unlikely to be the size of the financial benefit the multinationals are obtaining from operating in a virtual world, rather than in one where they have premises and offices and staff who pay taxes.

An associated question is, how long will it take to create the necessary legal disciplines? Moreover, what damage will the multinationals do to the international economy in the interim? It would be unlikely that their own national governments would be prepared to act against the interests of powerful international companies whose head office is located in the country, and presumably pays at least some tax. There needs to be a fundamental change to the basic global taxation principle that you have to have a permanent establishment in a country before you have to pay company tax.

2. Neutralise the effects of hybrid mismatch arrangements

New model treaty provisions and recommendations will be needed here. A 'hybrid mismatch' is no more than linguistic manipulation, whereby the same amount is regarded as a profit in one country and a loan in another.

***Comment*:** Until the industrial economies really start to feel the pain of profit shifting as it impedes their policy programs, especially as it hits their welfare and health budgets, the development of new treaty provisions will be a slow and vexed process. There are always national winners and losers in treaty negotiations, and there is no global force of compulsion that can require a country to act against the interests of its own citizens and of itself.

In the case of hybrid mismatches, a transaction should be simply described as what it is. A contorted misuse of language should not be able to alter the essential character of a cross-border transaction. It would be interesting to hear a judge's summation in a case where the plain English meaning of the language used to define a major tax concept was so contorted that profit and loans were taken to mean the same thing in two different jurisdictions, and the words actually used, 'hybrid mismatches', had no relevant meaning at all.

Higher courts generally look behind self-serving definitions and tortured expressions that don't use plain language.

3. Strengthen controlled foreign corporation rules

Controlled foreign corporation (CFC) rules are designed to limit artificial deferral of tax payments. The general taxation principle is that income is only taxed when a dividend is declared. Multinationals exploit this by simply borrowing against available dividends almost indefinitely or by not collecting outstanding debts owed by a subsidiary that has received relevant connected income. This commonly occurs with multinational subsidiaries whose parent company is in no hurry to collect the debt because it has to pay tax on the income or is cash rich.

Comment: This strategy is a simple way of disguising the real income that a multinational subsidiary has that has not been brought to account through dividends declared and tax paid. Working capital for the parent is never an issue, because lenders are aware of the existence of a fund of unpaid debts owed by subsidiaries that are always on call if the need ever arises. The other benefit is the opportunity to earn interest on the money without paying tax if the affiliate is in loss. This deferral has huge consequences for the national accounts of a country. No one knows the true balance-of-payments position.

4. Limit base erosion via interest deductions and other financial payments

Comment: This involves individual governments fine-tuning their domestic tax legislation to reduce unjustified or excessive financial payments and interest payments to overseas entities. It is very difficult for a tax authority to discriminate between genuinely justifiable financial costs and interest payments, and those made for transfer-pricing purposes. This is, of course, the nature of the present 'Dutch sandwich' arrangements which, with the connivance of some countries, disguise the final destination of payments. Few multinationals would be prepared to disclose their motives and arrangements to tax authorities that are not responsible to the government of the country where their head office is resident.

5. Counter harmful tax practices more effectively

Comment: This and several other of the OECD measures below are motherhood statements. They sound good, but have no specificity or substance. Some of them would have completion timelines of decades. The first task would be to define 'harmful'. Countering harmful tax practices is likely to be a task for global tax authorities into the next millennium.

5 (cont). Review country taxation regimes, including those in non-OECD countries

Comment: How will the OECD review tax regimes in countries that do not belong to the OECD? It is difficult to understand why those countries would co-operate if they regard their tax regime as positive in attracting international capital and investment, and providing a net financial benefit to the government and the country. And they may not want to join the OECD.

6. Prevent treaty abuse. Develop model treaty provisions regarding the design of domestic rules to prevent granting treaty benefits

Comment: Individual treaties have always taken many years to complete. The question is whether the major economies of the world and the OECD (in the face of what is truly a threat to the global economy) have the ability to act with some degree of urgency. The time lapse may be the terminal issue. The countries may consider that not joining the OECD is in their financial interest. The world has moved to a point where there is simply not enough time to proceed in the leisurely treaty-development fashion of the past. But how will the change come to pass without some concerted and relatively swift action?

7. Prevent the artificial avoidance of permanent-establishment status

Comment: This international problem may create conflict within the OECD. There is a precedent in the rise and demise of the global diplomatic corps. Until the 1990s, the diplomatic language was French, and clever corps staff moved around the world in a stately dance, from third secretary to chief of mission, which ended with Russia's *Glasnost* and *Perestroika*. The OECD may not be the twenty-first-century solution to the global problem of transfer pricing. Perhaps a global taskforce is needed, to consider and complete the plan in a world where time is of the essence. That, however, is unlikely.

8. Ensure that transfer-pricing outcomes are in line with value creation: intangibles

Comment: Valuing intangibles is obviously a complex task fraught with difficulty. Saying that something needs to be completed is not the same as completion.

PwC's Isabel Verlinden provided four basic steps for identifying intellectual property rights:

1. Identify intellectual property and the owners of the rights early. They are often scattered within a company or group.
2. Begin tax planning early in the intellectual-property life cycle when there is no documentation.
3. Link intellectual-property strategy to operational, commercial realities with sufficient substance.
4. Intangible valuations are not a one-off exercise. The value of the rights is volatile over time. Changes have to be recognised throughout the life cycle. For example, the brand name may become more valuable than the initial patents.

The strategy implicit in these steps is to value intangibles early and constantly to monitor and adjust their value as they move through the product lifecycle. (Their value diminishes towards the end of the lifecycle.) This is no easy task. At the early stages, value is often only in the mind of the creator. The calculations are no different from any product value that has a shifting monetary value from the time it begins to capture a market share to the time its market share declines — because new technology or a shift in consumer demand has made it unmarketable in the presence of competition from new products with greater performance or attraction. That is the usual character of the life cycle of durable consumer products, both large and small.

9. and 10. Ensure that transfer-pricing outcomes are in line with value creation for risks and capital, and other high-risk transactions

Comment: This is a daunting task that most multinationals have difficulty accomplishing themselves. It is important that whatever the OECD attempts should not be impossible to implement within a reasonable time frame. Until now, progress has been glacial. Little discipline has been applied to multinational practices for the past 25 years.

The task is a bit airy-fairy. Early in the lifecycle of a new product, the investing beholder or creator has a tendency to exaggerate the product's value. And few other people have the knowledge to determine the quantum of value involved in any transaction, let alone high-risk transactions. They lack the fundamental knowledge to make comparisons with other high-risk transactions. How can they measure value?

11. Establish methodologies to collect and analyse data on BEPS and associated actions

Comment: This will be a valuable exercise if OECD member countries can be persuaded truly to co-operate. It will be a substantial and difficult task.

12. Require taxpayers to disclose their aggressive tax-planning arrangements

Comment: How will the OECD achieve this? They have no legal authority to require taxpayers in the various countries to make disclosures. The tax authorities in each country have difficulty enough obtaining disclosure. The great enemy of national tax authorities is time and the stalemates they experience constantly when they seek disclosure from parties that have no obligation to respond to them. This seems an impossible task.

13. Re-examine transfer-pricing documentation

Comment: The process of examining transfer-pricing documentation has been in progress in OECD member countries and other countries for 25 years. It is not complete, but, as we have seen, the common methodology of choice, the transactional net margin method (TNMM), is being rejected by Australian courts. To some extent, higher court decisions should necessitate a review of the fundamental relevance of the TNMM. It is worthless to use methodologies that are clearly exposed to rejection by the courts.

The Australian court decisions may have impact on other jurisdictions, at least in so far as the arguments presented are examined. The existing TNMM documentation in Australia (which most multinational affiliates have used) at least has to be re-examined in the context of the retrospective legislation dating back to 1994 and the first Federal Court decision in favour of the ATO. The task is immense, and who will perform it with an independent mind? When this occurs, what will be the response of taxpayers who believed their past tax years had been closed and that they could proceed with present and future matters rather than constantly returning to past, closed issues?

The ATO now has the power to reopen closed years back to 2004, but it is obviously a vexed issue of principle. Retrospective legislation always initiates lengthy litigation if sufficient money is involved. This court outcome may involve a general ATO review of the TNMM if a company has, with the advice of the Big Four, used the TNMM, even if it had been accepted at the time by the ATO. The ultimate outcome of the Chevron case may answer this question, but any outcome is years away.

14. Make dispute-resolution mechanisms more effective

Comment: This is the ideal of virtually every government, court, and company. But, how do you do it? The OECD has the power to exclude members, but that is obviously a last resort. Again, time and the absence of legal authority prevent the OECD from imposing sanctions on countries that are not members.

15. Develop multinational instrument systems to enable jurisdictions to initiate measures relating to BEPS and amend bilateral trade agreements

Comment: Deadlines to the end of 2015 were suggested for the implementation of these measures. But it is likely to take a decade to develop, implement, and obtain member acceptance for the systems.

Finally, not listed by the OECD, but perhaps most importantly for Australia, the ATO should track the size of the problem and keep the measurement up to date. This may be wishful thinking, given the amount of data and the slowness of Schedule 25A receipts for international dealings from involved ATO clients and their advisers. The latest ATO update for related-party dealings was in 2013, and related to responses by companies in their Schedule 25A attachment to their tax returns for 2010–11. The ATO commented that Australian GDP in the 2011 year was $1.4 trillion, and that international trade between the related parties had a total value of $568 billion. However, Schedule 25A reports to the ATO were for a total of $269 billion, or less than half the actual value of trade between related parties. An accounting error of about a 100 per cent says something about the efficacy of Schedule 25A as a means of identifying the extent and nature of related-party dealings overseas.

The difficulty in evaluating international inter-company trade statistics and developing arguable positions on related-party dealings must not be underestimated. For 25 years, the ATO has been dealing with an avalanche of problems, a dearth of information, and a clever, educated, and very well paid group of transfer-pricing practitioners in the Big Four who have easy access to multinational lawyers and accountants who work globally for them.

The general problem with this wish-list of actions is that the OECD has no direct authority or even all-encompassing moral suasion to force or even encourage countries that are not OECD members to permit examinations of income involving companies resident in those countries. It cannot impose sanctions upon them requiring disclosures that the resident companies have no obligation to provide. The only possibility is that the country may be seeking to join the OECD and would need to be visited by its inspectors. If subsidiaries of multinationals operate in the country visited, this may provide some opportunity for suasion.

At the time of writing, the best that can be said for the OECD BEPS Action Plan is that some progress has been made through discussions, plans for the future, and unilateral responses by some countries on individual issues. These were probably the best immediate outcomes that could have been expected. The OECD has developed some ambitious time lines on individual issues for action:

Action Plan items 6, 7, and 10 were to be completed by the end of 2015. Step 6 concerns treaty abuse. The response from PwC was provided by Isabel Verlinden, whose comments included the following:

- 'Governments are also strapped for cash and are increasingly turning their attention to soft targets such as corporate tax revenues.'
- 'Consumers, the press and the broader public empowered by social media are scrutinising the corporate citizenship, governance, and practices — including tax practices — of the companies they buy from.'
- 'Tax policies should be coherent, consistent, reasonable and economically credible.'

These comments are self-serving. Corporate tax revenues are not a soft target for governments. If they were, a lot more tax would have been paid much faster in the past 25 years. In the Australian case, correlative relief and stonewalling would not have been used as tactics to bargain down the taxpayers' obligations to as little as one-third of the hundreds of millions of dollars that were calculated as payable in audit procedures that in some cases consumed years of audit, discussion, and settlement negotiations.

Essentially, the situation usually involved lengthy correlative-relief delays by the tax authority in the country of origin that had to adjust taxpayer payments to reflect their overpayment of tax there. To some extent, the Big Four's financial interest is intertwined with that of the multinationals. The Big Four sell time; and they sold a lot of that at very high prices to multinationals.

In these circumstances, it is easy to understand that governments are strapped for cash and will try to get multinationals to pay their fair share. They might not be so strapped if the transfer-pricing process was not so drawn out.

Given the facts and circumstances, and in the absence of any argument from the Big Four, it is difficult — in fact, intellectually offensive — to promote the view that this is merely an attack on corporate revenues by governments 'strapped for cash'. If in any case tax authorities had sought more than was payable, there would have been a court case rather than a settlement. There should have been no correlative-relief arguments that took years to settle after audits that themselves generally lasted for years. The official tax rates of the major corporations are known, and it is simple to calculate what tax should have been paid against the amount of tax that was paid.

During the interplay between the OECD and the Big Four over the OECD's BEPS Action Plan, PwC asserted that the world was now a digital economy and that the OECD could not prevent it. But the OECD isn't trying to stop internet selling. It is trying to create a mechanism for taxing the digital economy. That seems to be a pro-social outcome for the world. PwC reckons that it is impossible to tax the digital economy. It is wrong. Changes to the 'permanent establishment' concept to enable the taxation of companies with only virtual storefronts will be the likely mechanism in most instances.

PwC's statement is indicative of what is wrong with the self-serving analysis of what can be achieved to reform the tax grab of the past two decades. There is an almost religious fervour in the way the Big Four rationalise their taxation practices on the basis that those practices epitomise the new paradigm for world financial behaviour, and that this is a sufficient guarantee of their integrity. The fact is that most people in the world do not spend most of their time thinking about internet purchases or constantly trawling the internet. Buying online may be a preoccupation for a certain demographic in some developed countries, but we do not live in an internet world yet. The ancient Romans and Greeks bemoaned the fact that the youth of their time were convinced that they knew what was right and their elders didn't. In our time, the same conviction exists.

I suppose that the digital economy will just grow and grow until governments find a way to tax it at the levels that local taxpayers pay — those taxpayers who operate physical shopfronts and provide in-store and after-sales services, who hold physical stock and bear the cost of stock that does not sell or is returned. Speaking of which, spoiled or damaged stock is another problem. There is no international legislation that enables governments to force overseas sellers to pay refunds. Equally, buyers have no redress if dangerous goods cause them injury. There is no local affiliate with office holders who can be sued, fined, or, in serious matters, jailed.

The BEPS strategies listed below are only the tip of the iceberg of strategies used relentlessly by virtually all multinationals. Few have resiled from the temptation to do what the tax offices of the world have allowed them to do:

- Centralising regional management;
- Debt-financing subsidiaries in chronic debt (affiliates that may never have earned a profit since they were established in a country decades ago, and could never obtain a bank loan on an arm's-length basis);
- Using hybrid entities and financial instruments;
- Interposing conduit companies;
- Re-invoicing goods and services;
- Enabling base erosion through interest and financing transactions;
- Using preferential tax regimes in small and underdeveloped countries;
- Charging affiliates more than the arm's-length price for goods, services and intellectual property;
- Maintaining marketer-distributors in losses for years beyond what is possible for a stand-alone company; and
- Interposing a company that takes income from functions that are not tenable in arm's-length transactions.

Most of these concepts are defined by the OECD on its website.

September 2014: a line in the sand, or more Big Four humbug?

By the end of 2015, most countries would have considered the OECD BEPS Action Plan a major success. There had already been some major bloodless outcomes, such as the Irish government's decision to abolish the legislation that enabled the 'Double Irish'. Yet more than a year later, the substance of most major changes was still to occur.

Generally, the completion dates for submissions on the major items in the action plan were in 2015. But so far there has been no clarity regarding the attitude of the most important country in terms of parent multinationals, the United States. It seems to be in its best negotiating mode: agreeing to everything, but giving away nothing. Sometimes it fires a shot on a particular issue. Its views will only come to light when something is actually determined to be an OECD step that all countries should take. The Americans have launched no major BEPS offensive, but that might have been anticipated. A few Republican politicians and one assistant secretary in Treasury have been critical, but nothing more. It is difficult to defend the indefensible, and sometimes a slow stalemate accompanied by some soothing noises is sufficient strategy.

The discussions, the submissions, and the general air of conscientious co-operation in the OECD process on BEPS have drawn only a few obvious, jaundiced comments from the tax havens of Bermuda and Liechtenstein. But, to adapt Mandy Rice-Davies' words, said in other circumstances a long time ago, 'They would say that, wouldn't they?'

PwC has been emerging as the leading transfer-pricing practice among the Big Four for some years. Its contribution to the debate in its September 2014 newsletter was that virtually all the action plan items were under way. That *is* good to know. But it sounds a bit like the US's earnest commitments on climate change at the G20. What is under way is a lot of submissions, meetings, and further discussions.

The Big Four have made so much money in the past 25 years from transfer pricing that it is difficult to believe that they will scale back on their work to reduce tax for their multinational clients unless they find some other equally lucrative source of income. This statement is supported — in Appendix F — by comments from the UK parliamentary inquiry, alluded to in Chapter 20, that received submissions from each of the Big Four.

Conclusion

It is difficult to conceive of a complete solution to the problems created by multinationals that want to pay little or no tax. There are a lot of intermediate positions in transfer pricing, and little judicial review and commentary in the few decisions available internationally, let alone on a country-by-country basis.

The tax amounts volunteered by a few companies are risible when set against the enormous amounts of tax not paid. The contrast is shocking when expressed as a percentage and compared with the general tax levels paid by domestic companies (or, for that matter, the percentage of income tax the ordinary taxpayer pays in most major economies).

It would be interesting to know whether any one or even a few of the 600 companies in the Australian Large Business and International Group (that the ATO took over 20 years to review) paid the 30 per cent company tax rate. Evidence submitted in the recent Senate inquiry into tax avoidance showed that those pharmaceutical companies that had made advance pricing arrangements with the ATO had agreed to rates of around 30 per cent. Those that had no agreement were still paying single-figure tax rates. It is incomprehensible that pharmaceutical companies, all with much the same functions, assets, and risks, should be paying tax at such different rates.

More recently, the inquiry's interim report in April 2016 revealed the following:

> Apple Australia paid around $80 million in income tax on revenues of over $6 billion in 2013–14.
>
> From Australia's perspective, when Apple's Australian subsidiary sells an iPad for $600 to a customer in this country, it is estimated that about $550 (that is, approximately 90%) is shifted to Ireland. To make it worse, out of this $550, about $220 (that is, approximately 36%) is never taxed anywhere in the world. This is called 'double non-taxation' in the tax world.

Part of the global problem is that some major countries are benefiting from the transfer-pricing practices of multinationals and have actually created concessions to attract the multinationals (or at least their regional and head offices) to their countries. Switzerland, Hong Kong, Macau, Singapore, Malaysia, Ireland, and Holland are in that category. Most do not collect tax from companies resident in their country when income is earned outside the country. In any event, their general tax rates (including personal tax rates) are very low by world standards. The general academic response to the low-tax/no-tax strategy of these countries is that they are clever and industrious, rather than that they are parasites on what other nations are doing to provide welfare, education, infrastructure, democracy, and all those other expensive pro-social benefits.

The global financial crisis was a consequence of the incredible greed of the hot shots on Wall Street and their indifference to the damage they were doing as they pursued their own interest. The multinationals are no different from them. We are living in a time when the most powerful and knowledgeable financially among us are damaging our global economy and society, rather than contributing to it. How much money do they want? I think they just want 'more'.

Does anyone remember the Arthur Andersen accountancy firm? It employed, arguably, the strongest conceptual thinkers among what were then the Big Eight accountancy firms. Its accounting and business practices resulted in some of its partners going to jail, and the firm imploding and disappearing. What is different now?

There may ultimately be a similar accounting for the Big Four. The multinationals are not paying tax because their accountants have been able to obfuscate and delay the entire audit process internationally. No one, not even the Big Four, is defending this as a pro-social process. The consequences for society are simply ignored, even as the methodologies are defended.

The speed and number of global financial transactions today is frightening, and the rate is still accelerating to beyond warp speed. There are black holes in global stockmarket trading systems where sales and purchases can occur without any government or public scrutiny. They can be opened, closed, and completed in a millisecond. How can tax authorities determine the tax consequences of offshore trades that they don't even know are occurring? Audits of banks must be a nightmare for tax authorities, and presumably *are* for their external Big Four accountants.

Senior multinational executives should be required to divulge publicly the policy and procedures that inform their accounting practices. Why are they not required to divulge the total amounts owed to them by their subsidiaries and the ageing of the debts?

These hollow logs of money cast all over the world are simply created by the subsidiary not paying its parent or regional manufacturer for goods or services received until a time that is completely arbitrary when some debt is moved around. The multinationals and their regional offices in low-tax environments seem to be able to confine their responses to accounting concepts that have become archaic. What is needed in response is a bullshit filter that provides legally enforceable tax rulings and filters out the sort of judicial precedents that recommend the payment of zero or merely thousands of dollars of tax on many millions of dollars of income.

At public hearings, the spokespeople for the multinationals are nearly always lawyers or accountants. That was not true at the US Senate inquiries into the Global Financial Crisis. The presidents and vice-presidents of major companies were personally in the spotlight, answering questions. They could not sit back and let lawyers or junior staff respond to the questions. The multinational senior executives know and understand what has happened.

The GFC was an important harbinger for BEPS and transfer pricing. The intellectual mendacity of the Wall Street firms and their arrogance led to a global response that destroyed many careers, but did not reach quite deeply enough. Weasel words such as 'quantitative easing' are still being used to justify simply printing money and damaging the rest of the global economy just so the US can trade out of its hole. Those who lost hundreds of millions of dollars in the GFC have had little joy, as whatever funds remained have been substantially awarded in the first instance to US creditors (who got up to 30 per cent of their money back) by Delaware courts. The Australians were represented by very senior Australian legal counsel, but it made little difference. It may even have been counterproductive. The Australian creditors (including universities, councils, and superannuation funds) got less than 10 per cent of their money back.

The only GFC-related court victory for Australians that I know of occurred in February 2016, eight years after the event, when a substantial settlement was reached in a class action involving dozens of local councils and organisations relating to the collapse of Lehman Brothers Australia. The group had bought 'synthetic collaterised debt obligations' from Lehman Brothers Australia, and took the action against McGraw-Hill Financial and Standard & Poors, on the grounds that the ratings agency had misleadingly and deceptively assigned AA and AAA credit ratings to Lehman Brothers' products. This followed a successful Federal Court action three years previously, when the court found that the local Lehman Brothers company had engaged in misleading and deceptive conduct, breached its fiduciary duties, breached contracts, and acted negligently toward the plaintiffs.

We should try to get more hometown decisions in Australia in cases involving misrepresentations and losses resulting from the GFC. We certainly haven't got them from the US judiciary based in Delaware.

All the franchise and marketing agreements between Australian marketer-distributors and US brand-name owners were written within the context of the laws operating in the state of Delaware. I know because I wrote some of the agreements for Deloitte and Ernst & Young on behalf of the US multinationals in the late 1980s and early 1990s. I have also read many other agreements written in precisely the same terms.

Part of the BEPS solution for the Australian Tax Office may be to concentrate on the Big Four accounting firms and their behaviour in relation to the Institute of Chartered Accountants' Code of Ethics for Professional Conduct. As the situation stands,

Big Four clients are the targets of the OECD, and the Big Four are the advisers who engage the OECD and other tax authorities.

Until now, the ATO has focused entirely on the companies, and has not questioned the role of their advisers. The ATO and the Big Four seem too cosy for anyone's good. But who else deals with and understands transfer pricing? The ATO has no choice. Is it permissible for the Big Four to represent a company they know to be flouting or at least stretching the limits of accounting standards and rules? What position does the powerful Institute of Chartered Accountants (ICA) take on this?

It is worth noting that an institute of accountants exists in one form or another in all the major nations of the world. Clearly, some of the tax positions of the multinationals cannot be considered to be reasonable by any standard of professional conduct. For example, the ICA's own code of ethics looks beyond the simple tricks of some of the major companies operating totally in the internet space that have paid no tax at all simply because they have no permanent establishment in a country.

The view in the UK parliamentary committee of inquiry was that Big Four advisers who became consultants to the Tax Office were 'poachers who became gamekeepers who then became poachers again and exploited loopholes that they had created themselves when they were gamekeepers'. If this can be demonstrated to be true, why is this practice not a breach of the ICA's ethics code?

The same sort of infiltration by senior staff from the Big Four has occurred in the ATO. Ex-partners of the Big Four are now senior transfer-pricing advisers to the ATO. Senior tax officers, including people who had been assistant commissioners, have been recruited by the Big Four over the past 25 years at more than twice their ATO salaries. This is a major issue of integrity that does not seem to have worried the ATO in relation to senior staff, assistant commissioner, or partner movements either way between the ATO and the Big Four. Some of the movements (particularly from the ATO to the Big Four) were specifically for the purpose of dispute resolution.

The OECD BEPS initiative has been as successful as could be expected. The 15-point action plan has gone to various OECD committees that have included senior representatives from the Big Four. Some successes have already been achieved as some countries (including Ireland) have taken actions unilaterally. The program was supposed to have been completed by the end of 2016, but that was never going to happen.

Criticism of the BEPS initiative has been relatively limited. It appears to be a pro-social initiative in small countries that is almost impossible to dispute.

Taxing the digital economy does not seem as insoluble to me as a senior international PwC partner has suggested. Nor does the permanent-establishment issue seem to be that hard to overcome. What you have to do, as the song goes, is 'make everything old new again' — tax companies without a permanent establishment on the basis of the value of their imports. This is already happening in Europe with VAT charges for internet imports that are sold at cross-border prices beyond very low thresholds.

The direct-selling industry is a case in point. This is a multi-billion-dollar global industry of about 90 companies — including Avon, Amway, Nutrimetics, and Herbalife — who often pay little or no tax because they operate without permanent establishments, and because the revenue received by its marketers, the direct-sales people, is usually below a taxable level. In Australia, this represents a sales force of around 400,000 people who pay no tax at all. Clearly, such overseas companies should be required to have a permanent establishment in Australia.

There needs to be joint action by the G9 and G20 to agree to common tax processes and principles that are applied to all member countries, just as the Brussels Nomenclature was applied over one hundred years ago.

The biggest losers in the digital global economy are the poorest people in low-income countries. These countries are the new, nation-sized versions of the sweatshops of the twentieth century. Their countries have become the new havens for profit shifting. It is difficult to imagine what can be done in circumstances where the meagre income of the poorest and most numerous segment of the population is so precarious. Their governments are willing to legislate and take what they can get as income for acting as service centres for the multinationals. The governments are paid a relative pittance for that permission, and the workers performing back-office functions in the service centres get less than a pittance.

This issue is socially sensitive. Overseas call-centre workers are poorly paid, but that meagre income is crucial to them. They are almost hostages in the process. There is no shortage of people ready to replace them for the same payment or even less.

The issue is not just clever tricks with tax. It is social justice. Transfer pricing has become a global monster that threatens the social fabric of the entire world.

Part III
Australia: a case study

Introduction

Even in the absence of transfer pricing, multinational corporations would still have driven virtually all local manufacturers of goods out of their national markets. Services are a more complex area of the market, though even there the multinationals have captured most of the supply chain for marketing and after-sales services that relate to their own products. Some major retailers are multinationals in their own right. For this reason, the entry of some international marketers to the Australian market (for example, Aldi) has not been welcomed by companies such as Coles.

Multinationals simply have the financial capability, scale of production, and intellectual property that must exist to underpin globally significant product development and manufacturing technology. Often they have been successful product innovators, developers, and disseminators for more than a century, and have had access to any amount of development capital they may have required. They also dominate the global internet market for goods and services.

The availability of strategies to minimise or eliminate taxes on income, and the ability and willingness of multinationals to implement these strategies, have shortened their development-to-market lifecycle. Local companies have been driven from national markets by the multinationals' immense competitive advantage in intellectual-property ownership, massive funds availability, and economies of scale of operations, and by the fact that they pay little if any income tax in many major markets. Local companies are at a major strategic disadvantage because they pay tax at the legislated rates.

The simple truth is that there are virtually no Australian multinational corporations. A few mining companies would come the closest. That single reality is the great tragedy of the Australian economy. It is likely to be the reason why the Australian economy and standard of living will decline once our reserves of minerals and other raw materials are either depleted or their ownership passes to citizens and companies of other nations. Our land is being sold so that even agricultural production is falling into foreign hands. Eventually, we will become the tenants of a country owned by (mostly) absentee landlords.

The great, strategic, competitive error of our leaders and thinkers has been to cling to patently false economic theories of free trade. In Australia, we have dismantled the industries that other nations have spent centuries developing in their home markets in the first instance and then have migrated to overseas markets. That development included manufacturing industries and companies that add value to raw materials and create global brand names. The United States, Europe, Japan, and Korea are the global owners of the intellectual property and brand names for manufactured goods. Australia is just another raw materials and foodstuffs supplier in the global market. We add no value to our abundant raw materials.

Most industrial economies got rid of tariffs in the 1980s, but only Australia and New Zealand dismantled non-tariff mechanisms and domestic industry protection as well. Europe, the US, China, and Korea realised that non-tariff barriers were more effective and certainly more politically acceptable. Such assistance mechanisms and barriers live on in the individual state legislations of the US. The US–Australia free-trade agreement has been implemented by only a few US states.

Some of the best and brightest Australians are senior executives in multinational management. The ancient precedents for this are well known. Greek slaves ultimately ruled the Roman Empire. They were not the owners, but obtained power through their ability to manage the empire while the Romans plotted and partied. The next level of Australian executives (those on the next step down on the corporate ladder) often work in Asian low-tax environments. It is a strong attraction for couples when they both work and are enthusiastic about their careers. Many would see the situation as a career opportunity, a comfortable lifestyle, and a way of saving enough money from a low-tax income to buy a home.

Many talented and ambitious Australian men and women working in Singapore, China, and Hong Kong aspire to head-office jobs in Europe or the US. The jobs in low-tax regional offices are important (and a wonderful child-care solution if both parents work), but their aspiration is to be part of the global senior executive network or the senior management team in the parent company's home base.

The multinationals' domination of national economies

In his novel *The Trouble with Lichen*, English author John Wyndham (also author of *The Day of the Triffids*) wrote about the catastrophic effects for civilisation of the discovery of a species of lichen in the Himalayas. It seemed at first to be a boon for mankind: consumption of the lichen enabled users to live to 700 years of age. The difficulty was that the lichen was an extremely rare commodity, and few people could afford to buy it. Other problems quickly emerged. Insurance companies with superannuation policies based on actuarial studies of life expectancies quickly went bankrupt. Few marriages could survive for 50 years, let alone 500. Children never inherited, and would always die before parents who had spent the children's inheritance on lichen.

The reality of this parable is being demonstrated today when ageing parents in Australia often sell the family home to pay for their own or their spouse's care in a nursing home. We haven't got to Wyndham's situation yet, but there is often a lot of angst among young married and middle-aged children in the present day when the family home is sold to maintain an aged parent's care in an upmarket nursing home. In situations where the husband dies first, the grandmother often spends the inheritance on school fees for the grandchildren.

In *The Trouble with Lichen*, the ultimate results of the discovery of lichen were murder and riots. Children, faced with the likelihood that they would grow old and die long before their parents, because they couldn't afford to buy lichen, murdered them. There were lichen riots when the people believed that government ministers were hoarding lichen for themselves.

The tax practices of multinationals, and the looming financial and social disaster for developed economies, have real-life parallels to Wyndham's lichen fable. The multinationals have generally extinguished competition arising from small (or even reasonably large) competitors in nearly 200 global markets, and either pay less tax than national legislators intended they should pay to support social services, or pay no tax at all.

Ultimately, governments will not have the financial capacity to support an ageing population that can no longer find paying work.

The unemployed might riot if they have no food or shelter, and no likelihood of better days for themselves or their children. The social consequences for Australia of the long-term continuation of the multinationals' failure to pay a fair share of tax are discussed in the final part of this book. We are a uniquely endowed nation that was once correctly described as a small, rich, industrial country. That description no longer applies.

Australia has no value-adding industries, and our current-account deficit has continued to grow even during the biggest mining boom we have ever had. As the boom ends, the future looks grim unless governments discard the free-market economic model that has held sway in Australia for the past 40 years. The fact is that Australia is rapidly being impoverished by the never-ending, constantly growing current-account deficit and a level of disguised unemployment that is being supported by the sale of our assets and the operation of Centrelink.

Centrelink is a huge, benign poorhouse that supports those who are too old, too uneducated, too unskilled and, increasingly often, too unable to communicate because of inadequate English. Our pension-aged population enjoys its independence in flats and other low-rent accommodation. They at least have the liberty to choose where they live, and have the ability to pay for it with the pension.

Up until the 1970s, the pension was the ultimate panacea of Australia's working class. Men who smoked (and they were in the majority) often didn't bother the public purse for as much as 10 years after they retired. Centrelink today manages a new generation of social programs that replaces what was the Australian age pension. It is a much broader system that extends to a much wider group of people in need. Centrelink spends about 10 per cent of Australia's national budget each year. As life expectancy and our migrant intake increases, it will spend more.

Although the owners of the multinational corporations are citizens of Europe, Asia, and the United States, their wealth and power is not distributed widely among the population, and is seldom brought home. The company owners and senior executives are becoming citizens of the world. The latter may spend their lives as part of a senior executive group within the corporation, and live in six or seven major markets for some years at each location.

Multinational affluence is concentrated in relatively few hands, and is mobile internationally. The multinationals that are the owners of intellectual property are the major global policy and financial decision-makers, even if their accumulated funds are scattered in tax havens. They can access funds in the overseas debtor accounts of their subsidiaries at any time. Although the money doesn't move physically, the multinational's ownership of it is sufficient for global banks to extend funds to their global affiliates for many years (in some cases, decades), supported only by letters of comfort from the parent companies.

Asia and China have a huge underclass that is likely always to live in poverty. The US is in the same situation with Mexicans, African-Americans, and Asians who are often employed in menial occupations.

That has not been the case in Australia. With the exception of our original population, there has not been an underclass in Australia until recently. The 1950s and 1960s were the era when most youths left school after nine years of education to work in the trades or, in the case of women, as teachers, typists, shop assistants, bank clerks, and administration officers in the federal and state public service, or in councils and in state clerical and administrative functions. Many were employed by Woolworths and Coles, or other retail outlets. Universities were too expensive — their annual fees were almost as much as the average working wage for a year. Most peoples' ambition was to own a home and bring up a family.

Global company dominance and the consequent Australian diaspora

Over the past 25 years, a major market change has occurred in the industrialised countries of the world. It is a change driven by a major attack on the tax foundations and markets of the industrialised economies. Australia, that 'small, rich, industrial country', is an example of the damaging power that can be exerted by multinationals that decide to pay as little tax as possible, and have developed, with their Big Four accounting advisers, the accounting strategies and means to achieve that goal.

Where multinationals are involved in significant product manufacture, one major instrument of tax avoidance is their use of global buying chains. They often source components and semi-manufactured items from underdeveloped countries, and assemble them in China, India, Indonesia, or other low-wage economies that give the multinational the ability to avoid tax almost totally.

Multinationals have changed the character of our global civilisation. They may have originated in a particular country 100 or more years ago, but they are practically stateless now. US President Barack Obama has been a strident critic of the risible amount of tax that home-grown multinationals pay in the US. The internet multinationals are much more recent, and their business model is a new tax phenomenon: they are literally stateless, and often pay no tax. Their ability to be businesses without having permanent establishments has generally placed them outside the relevant provisions of the often outdated tax legislation of most countries. This means they can engineer their tax commitments in several countries to pay, in some cases, no tax at all, or only a risible amount.

The contempt for the pro-social taxation policies of the countries where they originate and now market and sell is obvious. However, this is now being politely but emphatically exposed by the OECD's Action Plan on BEPS. The fundamental question the OECD is posing the multinationals is whether they are changing the world economy for better or worse.

The positive contribution of multinationals has been their financial strength and willingness to undertake research and development to create global consumer products. Many of these products have increased both the quality of life and its length.

To some extent, this book is a lament for an Australian society that has gone, and a genuflection to that past society and its core values. Australia is moving into an age where there will be a new, sharp division within society that is not created by age, health, intellect, or education. Our population will be much more multicultural, and many newcomers will struggle for employment in anything except menial jobs. As in the past, their children will benefit from the struggles of their parents and their access to free education, at least until the end of school — though I doubt whether the upward mobility of past migrants will be matched by present child migrants and the young children of present migrants. Regrettably, some doors have closed or been sealed up. Australia's unique, classless society has gone. Membership of the new Australian social plutocracy is defined by wealth. Jack will no longer be as good as his master. Those who work at senior levels for the multinationals or own a substantial share portfolio in them will be the social glitterati.

Transfer pricing, the annihilation of value adding in

Australia, increased life expectancy, and a population explosion, in combination with a rapidly disintegrating work ethic and excessive and sometimes very wasteful consumption, are shaping as the Economic Horsemen of the Apocalypse for Australia in the next 30 years.

Yet there is hope. Some changes are been made that are creating a more competitive Australia. However, none of these changes are consequences of government policy or the mantras of productivity improvement and innovation of the past 30 years.

Someone (ideally, within the federal government, with its mishmash of departments and authorities that all own a piece of the data jigsaw puzzle that must be assembled) should complete a stocktake and prepare a national balance sheet of Australia's assets and liabilities. That might be the first step in a national strategy that goes beyond individual, short-term, and state interests.

'Productivity and innovation' was the policy chorus for more than 20 years, though the genuine long-term successes were sparse. Today it is apparent that governments of both political parties achieved little other than forcing millions of people to ask Centrelink for a pension or unemployment benefits because their jobs had disappeared.

How many other countries spend 10 per cent of their income on the unemployed, and another 10 per cent on compulsory superannuation? The answer is none. Right now, Paul Keating is championing a major political move to increase the compulsory superannuation rate to 15 per cent. Many former Labor Party luminaries and senior apparatchiks are deeply involved in the management or guardianship of superannuation funds. There has been some recent public disquiet about that.

Similarly, how many people are employed by councils, state governments, and the federal government? We have never calculated how many people are employed in the three levels of government. Finally, the great cost to federal and state governments (and councils) of the services of consultants who were previously public servants, council members, or trade union officials also should be public. The salary of a permanent head of department is now approaching $900,000 a year.

Lots of other entities should be included in any tally of Australia's non-productive workforce. The manufacturing sector of the Australian economy has shrunk from 25 to 7 per cent, and most federal bureaucrats think that is a good thing.

Our assets

Australia is a multicultural society in a state of flux that we are still bedding down. Most of our Asian migrants are young, clever, and industrious. Our reserves of iron ore, coal, and gold obviously have a finite life. Kalgoorlie and Coolgardie were the richest goldmines in the world in the late nineteenth century, but the ore has been extracted now, and the towns are shadows of what they once were. In any case, the extraction of iron ore and coal employs no more than a fraction of the population in Western Australia and South Australia. The international price of iron ore has declined rapidly since the second half of 2014.

Australia is a huge country that is clean and green. We have yet to fully exploit that competitive advantage. We haven't sold all of it yet. Quarantine policy over the past 50 years means that Australia has remained free of the crop and livestock diseases that have plagued other countries.

Our liabilities

Welcome to the Banana Republic of Australia. There have been too many bushranger billionaires and corrupt politicians, union officials, and policemen that I have been involved with. I've also dealt with state and federal governments for nearly 50 years. That exposure to politicians, plutocrats, public servants, and lawyers is the experience underlying my conclusions.

Australia simply has too many levels of government. Bob Hawke, our long-serving prime minister in the 1980s, delivered the Boyer Lecture in 1979. Sir Richard Boyer was a chairman of the ABC for a long time, and his son Richard was a commissioner in the Industries Assistance Commission, which subsequently became the Productivity Commission in 1998. Hawke's thesis was that we should get rid of one level of government. He was right. We have hundreds of district and regional councils, state governments, and a federal parliament comprising a House of Representatives and a Senate.

All Australia's state governments (except Queensland) also have upper houses, which are British hangovers from the division between the people's parliament and the unelected house where those of noble birth could prevent or amend legislation passed up from the people's parliament. No one is sure what value the upper houses add to the government process.

The state upper houses are complete anachronisms. They are not representative of the will of the people, and seem to contribute very little to the process of legislative review. The federal Senate has also degenerated, simply because the electoral process in place for decades was allowed to continue and was ultimately corrupted completely by very small (micro) parties and their advisers gaming the preference-distribution system. This rort, at least, was removed before the 2016 double-dissolution election was triggered.

The real problem has been the long-known opportunity to game preferences to permit Senate selection of individuals from parties that represent a minute fragment of the voting population.

At the federal level, the media have been more interested in the personal shenanigans that have included direct conflicts between leaders and followers in minor parties, making complete nonsense of the policy foundations (such as they were) that got them elected. As the media has revelled in these personal conflicts, it has ignored the consequences for Australian political processes and policies, and its national purpose — and that is tragic.

Virtually every state government in the past 30 years has been involved in venal scandals and corruption that have consumed thousands of hours of inquiries which seem to end without any real punishment, other than the minister or senior parliamentarian losing (or resigning from) their seat in the state parliament. They walk away with a fortune won corruptly and, possibly, a lifetime state pension.

Then there are the Productivity Commission, the Reserve Bank of Australia, and a cluster of federal and state government authorities, Centrelink, and a gaggle of public/private enterprises. The first two agencies have long histories, but seem to have lost their direction. The Reserve Bank seems to be almost exclusively focused on the interest rate. It has a magnificent library, and maintains important databases of statistics relating to the Australian financial market. But the bank is a club at which virtually all the assistant governors have worked for their entire working lives. They are internationalists who do not seem to want to deal with Australian issues beyond the base interest rate. That rate only applies to large institutions and major companies such as banks. It has stagnated in recent years.

The early education of the assistant governors has generally involved a brainwashing at Harvard and the inculcation of a global/US view of the central bank's philosophy and functions. The UK used a similar tactic very successfully when Cecil Rhodes created his generous scholarships that allowed clever Empire ploughboys to go to Oxford and develop an appropriate sense of the importance of the British Empire and the way it should be ruled. The US elite of New York, Washington, and Boston have followed this strategy as a way of creating power and influence in other nations. The Australian approach has been the same. It is not about your talents or experience; it is about your attitude. Independent thinkers need not apply.

In my late twenties (that is, in the early 1970s), I was invited by strangers (apparently with credentials and connections) to fly to Melbourne to meet the American ambassador, though no agenda was proposed for discussion. The strangers paid my fare and accommodation. Out of curiosity (and good manners), I went to the meeting. It was an interesting discussion with a group of 10 men. The ambassador said nothing. I had never met anyone who was there, and they did most of the talking. My few comments did not please them. Some of the things I said seemed to enrage them. The debate was hot on a few occasions. I was never invited to meet them again.

At about the same time, I had a similar social experience at the Commonwealth Club in Canberra, where I met three of the Australian Public Service (APS) heads, including the heads of Treasury and the APS. They were all knights of the realm. Again, that was a meeting at which the commissioner who had set up the meeting with me said nothing, while the rest asked for my opinions. I think this was to determine whether I was the 'right type' to be an assistant commissioner with prospects. That was a positive meeting, but I left the public service anyway.

This selection process struck me as elitist and antiquated. I don't believe that advancement should be based upon being 'one of the team' in your thinking. That was clearly the case in the Industries Assistance Commission, Treasury, and the Prime Minister's Department.

But sometimes it's a good idea to have a few independent thinkers around.

CHAPTER THIRTEEN

Is Australia history?

Most Australians who grew up in the 1950s and 1960s had an inferiority complex. The United Kingdom was still home for the upper classes, and everyone else was a Reffo, a Wog, or a Dago (that is, a refugee) from somewhere in Europe who lived in the inner suburbs of Sydney and Melbourne, or out in the back suburbs where three-bedroom family homes were still being built. The general attitude was that Australia was a suitable final destination for the refuse of Europe.

Nearly all Australian children left school when they were 15 years of age with what was called the Intermediate Certificate. Only the rich could afford to go to university. The fees were £1,000 a year, which was the amount the average worker earned in a year in the 1960s. Scholarships were rare.

The rise and demise of Australia's manufacturing industry

In the 1950s, a few outstanding Australian engineers persuaded General Motors in the United States to provide the intellectual property to start manufacturing cars in Australia. That encouraged GM's great competitor, Ford, also to establish a manufacturing plant in Australia. In the 1960s, Nissan and Toyota also began manufacture. A welcome spinoff was a thriving components industry that eventually involved over 300 producers. At its peak, the motor industry employed 200,000 people in Victoria, New South Wales, and South Australia. They have nearly all left the industry now, and those few who remain will be leaving soon. The Productivity Commission's mantra has always been that the unemployed will be employed in more efficient, competitive occupations. I wonder how many of them will end up at Centrelink for the rest of their working lives (and the rest of their lives, for that matter).

The Australian textiles, clothing, and footwear industry employed 200,000 people, and it disappeared with the same rationale from the commission. Tariffs and quotas were abolished, and none of the non-tariff forms of protection used in other countries was substituted.

Once the owners of brand names worked out that they could establish manufacturing facilities in China and other low-labour-cost countries with perfect replication and zero defects, all they had to own was the intellectual property, and the income could be collected in a low-tax or no-tax locations.

There has never been any substantial demographic study of what happened to the displaced employees in the car, and textiles, clothing, and footwear industries. Where did the employees live? Did they obtain other employment? Or did most of them go to Centrelink and become a permanent impost upon Australia's social services system for decades?

It might have been instructive for the Productivity Commission and other major government departments to learn of the long-term outcome of the employee dislocation and its cost to the Australian economy. After all, the commission and key departments were the architects of the demise of the industry. An examination of Centrelink's customer growth — their origins, family size, and duration on benefits — and the consequential increasing funding demands upon the Australian government's budget over the past 20 years, would also be valuable.

As we have seen, the rise and rise of transfer pricing over the past 25 years is directly connected to the fall in customs duty rates. Our hidden unemployment, the growth of part-time employment, the increasing movement of women into the workforce, mostly on a part-time basis, with the concomitant struggle to pay for adequate child care, and other dysfunctional impacts on families, are all, to some extent, a consequence of the decline in the manufacturing sector and its knock-on effects on supplier industries.

Australia and the Asian diaspora

In many nations there are times when the passing of a way of life is evident. There is a shift from the character and principles of a society that cannot be reversed. It happened in the US after the destruction of the South in the Civil War. It happened again in the UK with the annihilation of a generation of young men as they went over the top of the Belgian and French trenches of World War I into gas, huge shells fired from 20 kilometres away, and enfilades of machine guns. It all happened again in World War II. It happened to Japan with the dropping of the atomic bombs. Australia has managed to avoid much of the direct impact of those catastrophes, though we were certainly grievously hurt by the European wars and the war with Japan.

The present Australian catharsis has been different. Our society has been changing bloodlessly. By 2016, Australia was becoming part of the Asian diaspora. That global sense of national identity wherever you may live has been a major bonding force for Greeks, Jews, Italians, and Chinese migrants scattered throughout the world. For too long, we were shackled by the idea that we were a neglected outpost of the British Empire, but that the empire would look after us. Eventually, the UK cut the apron strings (without bothering to ask our permission), and we are now heading in another, logical direction. Asia is a lot closer to us than Europe, and perhaps a lot more interested in what Australia has to offer for the future.

The rise and rise of China and the decline of European trade is positive for Australia from a balance-of-trade and exports perspective. We are no longer merely at the end of the supply chain, and a substantial population of young Chinese entrepreneurs have moved to Australia. They are the major textiles, clothing, and footwear importers in the market. Their ability to negotiate directly with Chinese manufacturers and exporters is a huge benefit. In the past, there was little opportunity to negotiate, because Australian volumes commanded no respect or even interest from Chinese suppliers focused on their markets in Europe and the US. Moreover, their seasons were the reverse of ours.

In the late 1980s I acted as a consultant to Coles for some years. Coles belonged to a lobbying group (the Australian Exporters and Importers Group) I created to seek periodic customs entry rather than having to seek entry for every single shipment of the same goods for the same importer, as had been the requirement since Federation and is to this day.

An executive of Coles who had been a Customs officer for over 20 years told me that Coles bought clothing from Asian manufacturers that had been manufactured in production runs for the Northern Hemisphere markets of Europe and North America. Australia might order 2,000 garments while the other customers were ordering 100,000 each. The garments came in bags with tags, and were simply stored for a few months until the spring sales. It was the only way to be even able to place an order at the major textile and clothing mills of China.

Australia has spasmodically attempted to exploit its clean, isolated, island advantage. In the 1980s, an annual report from what is now called the Productivity Commission included as its major policy discussion the promotion of Australia as the clean, green, pest-free food bowl for Asia. However, that quest seems to have foundered as a consequence of bureaucratic logistics problems and overseas border barriers. Asia's governments protect their industries with non-tariff barriers.

We have that clean, green reputation for food because of our almost globally unique quarantine rules (which have been slightly relaxed in the past 20 years). It may be that our long-term opportunity with China is to send it processed meat, cereals, dairy products, and vegetables — instead of coal and iron ore. This opportunity certainly offers a substantial area of trade that the young Chinese entrepreneurs at present working between China and Australia in the consumer-goods and textiles industries could capture. Some of those people seem to move seamlessly between Australia and China.

We have just signed a free-trade agreement with China, after nine years of negotiations. It may not be an all-encompassing agreement, but at least it provides for a focus on Asia that takes in more than minerals and other raw materials. At least the entrepreneurs in the Australian mining industry will have created profitable connections in China.

The European and US founders of multinational corporations are not the only breed of entrepreneurs in the world. The business models they created and their strategies of paying as little tax as possible are simply a very large version of the standard philosophy that is still in use among the Asian entrepreneurs in Australia who came here less than 50 years ago. That often involves saving cash receipts and keeping them out of sight of tax officers.

Globally, the social tragedy created by this process is obvious and chilling. The historical upstairs-downstairs phenomenon of humanity falling into classes according to whether they are rich or poor happened in Australia almost from early-settler times. There has always been a divide between the city and the country. There is also a divide between the inner and the outer suburbs: between those living in Vaucluse or Double Bay, and those trying to live at Green Valley or in the unreconstructed parts of inner Sydney.

Additionally, quick-witted or lucky and well-connected country kids have always moved to the city, leaving Dad and Mum on the farm. These young people get high-paying jobs. Youth unemployment is extremely high in regional areas and towns. On the other hand, many young people from the richer suburbs benefit from the networking of their affluent parents at school, in their companies, and at golf courses and clubs.

How many Australian families will spend their lives out of work, living in poverty and under constant threat of financial disaster? The providers of services such as gas, water, and electricity are corporations now. They act as corporations do, and turn off the electricity, turn off the gas, and evict tenants who haven't paid their rent. In the event of a dispute over what may be an excessive bill, they are never wrong. The days of the state housing commissions are long gone. Where there was social dysfunction, particularly with unemployed alcoholic parents, they tried to show compassion and a social conscience.

Australians are not all equal any more. The days of the Greek and Italian milk bar, fishermen, and fruit-shop entrepreneurs are finished. Many young people see no real opportunity to succeed with the tactics their parents used: plain hard work and common sense over a lifetime. Many of the young are alienated by a system that is based on intellect, education, and connections rather than integrity, decency, and hard work. They are disciples of global brand names, particularly in fashion. They will not wait for anything.

The passing of twentieth-century Australia

The introduction of sea freight containers in the 1960s, and air freight in the 1990s, and the elimination almost entirely of tariff and quota barriers (and any other form of non-tariff and state government assistance) by the early 1990s were the events that enabled the major penetrations of the Australian market.

Between the early 1970s and the 1990s, tariffs and quotas were reviewed, and then removed or massively reduced. This ended a process that had originated with the Tariff Board in 1927. At that time, the board was full of protectionists, so named because they saw their role as protecting Australian manufacturers from cheap imports. Alf Rattigan became chairman in the 1960s and presided over a massive reduction in quotas and tariff levels in the 1970s that was innocently named 'The Tariff Review'.

The Tariff Board was renamed the Industries Assistance Commission (IAC) in 1974, then the government dropped the word 'assistance' and we had the Industries Commission. Its ultimate, Orwellian name is the Productivity Commission. The commission hasn't done a single, memorable thing to improve productivity in Australia in the past 30 years.

From the time of the IAC onwards, little assistance to industry has been forthcoming from the commission. Its role was to reduce tariffs and get rid of quotas. The activities of the commission are now totally removed from manufacturing-industry issues and public inquiries.

Since the early years of the twenty-first century, China has increasingly dominated the Australian market for textiles, clothing, and footwear, and (as the Japanese did previously) other consumer goods. China has changed the sources of supply for a broad range of consumer goods for most global markets. These changes have resulted in the annihilation of local manufacturers and retailers that could not adapt to what is a very efficient and fast 'international-to-domestic-market', end-to-end supply-chain. It has made imports from Asia to Australia much more competitive against imports from Europe and America.

Our mineral exports have benefited from our relative proximity to the markets of China, Korea, and Japan. Our major competitors are in South America, and they face their own 'tyranny of distance' when shipping raw materials to Asia.

Australian manufacturers (those few that are left) do not own the global brand names or possess the scale of production, media reach, and logistics economies that would allow them to compete and differentiate their product in the marketplace. On the rare occasions that they do compete successfully, the business has been quickly sold offshore. That is a great tactic to get rid of genuine competition.

The Australian business environment is littered with examples of overseas companies that have employed the base-erosion and profit-shifting strategy. Multinational affiliates that were manufacturers are now marketer-distributors. They have generally been able to keep their multi-year tax losses when they ceased local production and changed their business model from manufacturers to importers and marketer-distributors. This has happened with motor-vehicle manufacturers; they have already transitioned to being marketer-distributers. It also happened with most main street retailers of luxury goods that moved offshore and now trade solely on the internet —particularly, marketers of cosmetics, toiletries, and fragrances. Soon, the last two foreign-owned carmakers in Australia (Toyota and Holden) will be reborn as marketer-distributors. They are classic examples of BEPS at work.

In the past, car companies had to homologate car models to meet Australian design rules. That often cost millions of dollars, and was a form of non-tariff protection that forced the overseas manufacturers to have short production runs for Australia or to set up in Australia. They will not do that anymore. The size of the Australian market and the number of models competing in it will not support that manufacturing equation. Holden and Toyota's imported models will dominate the Australian motor-vehicle market and the aftersales market for years. It will be very profitable, but they will be able to offset their existing tax losses against the profits.

The essential justification and process for BEPS is simply explained. The parent company begins in a market by using distributors to test the market response. Then subsidiaries begin manufacturing, with government grants and/or tariff and quota walls. Once the market is established and the brand name embedded, it is time for BEPS and low-cost manufacturing in an Asian country that does not tax foreign-sourced income.

It was inevitable that BEPS would come to Australia. We are too far away from major markets other than China, Japan, and Korea. Our labour force is paid much more than the workers in those countries. Finally, other countries look after their own manufacturers, but are happy to buy commodities and raw materials to which they can add value. They have non-tariff barriers when they have domestic manufacturers.

We also fell in love with the notion of free trade. The Australian Public Service mandarins who were chairmen of the

Tariff Board through its reincarnations as the IAC and then the Productivity Commission were the ultimate true believers in free trade. After their retirement, two chairmen of the authority who held office during its passage from Tariff Board to Productivity Commission (Bill Carmichael and Alf Rattigan) wrote a book promoting the idea that the unilateral trade reduction of duties to zero was a good idea, even if the rest of the world did not follow suit. (It still hasn't.) It is difficult to remember anyone else in their position who had such incredible hubris, and pursued the exact antithesis of their work charter. It is also incredible that no academic or senior policy mandarin stood up and ridiculed the book.

Some European countries continue to maintain non-tariff barriers. There aren't many Fiats in France, or Renaults in Italy. Equally, in Asia, you won't buy a Suntory beer in Korea, given the price advantage of Korean beer (or even the price of European and American beers relative to the price of Korean brands). Japan has been a master of non-tariff barriers, especially those that involve leaving imports on the port docks or in the wharf warehouses for years. American carmakers are periodically outraged by non-tariff barriers in Europe, although American and European carmakers (and Japanese, for that matter) are almost all shareholders in each other's companies now.

One famous, long-dead parliamentarian is still wrongly remembered by a group of Australian Liberals as the great champion of zero tariffs. Bert Kelly (the member for Wakefield) wrote a book called *One More Nail* and had a column in *The Australian Financial Review* for years. I went to see him at his home in Adelaide after his book was published. Of course, Kelly just wanted the tariffs to be lower than they were in the 1960s, 1970s, and 1980s. He would have objected strongly to zero rates.

Years later, *The Australian Financial Review* published a letter of mine quoting exactly what Kelly had said in parliament about tariffs. He had wanted lower tariffs, not zero tariffs. He objected to percentage tariff rates in the 30s and 40s or higher, especially when there were other protective mechanisms at both the state and federal levels. Moreover, these tariffs were often imposed on goods where there was no local manufacturer.

The only opinion leaders who wanted zero tariffs were ideologues in the Treasury and the Productivity Commission, their political acolytes, self-interested multinationals, and starry-eyed commentators in the finance sector. None of them knew or cared about the real-world consequences of their prejudices.

CHAPTER FOURTEEN

The end of distance

Where we came from and what earlier Australians did are matters of history. We should learn from history. Our recent past and present performance have not been, to use the Australian vernacular, too flash. If you spend your life either watching Australian politics or trying to engage with the politicians, police, public servants, and plutocrats, you feel very dissatisfied as you reach the final act.

Australia's parliamentarian and union officials' chicanery is possibly the most corrupt in the Western world (at least in its longevity and focus on non-drugs-based corruption). In the past decade, every state government has been embroiled in scandalous favours and contracts (that are financially rewarded) for their mates. It's the Australian way.

I suppose we are all grandchildren of Ned Kelly, or fellow travellers with Machiavelli.

The most important question is, where is Australia going? We won't remain a big, rich, mineral, and agricultural country forever. The historical spectre of the impoverishment of South America is instructive. Brazil and Argentina were economies rich in precious minerals, and had major rural industries. They were a long way from anywhere, except the United States. That model doesn't work in the twenty-first century.

Our melting-pot immigration moments (since World War II) are also more recent than the nineteenth-century experience of the US. We had no slaves, but on many occasions we employed hunting parties to engage in the wholesale slaughter of the indigenous people, and even since then we have not found out how to treat them well or look after their interests. They are our equivalent of the native Americans.

Australia's Asian future

In 1984, Professor Geoffrey Blainey (the author of *The Tyranny of Distance*) was on the wrong side of the racial debate when he stated (to a meeting of a thousand Rotarians at Warrnambool):

> I do not accept the view, widely held in the Federal Cabinet, that some kind of slow Asian takeover of Australia is inevitable. I do not believe that we are powerless.
>
> Australia to be a nation worth living in must be *monocultural* as well as multicultural. It must possess shared values as well as different values.

Blainey also said that the pace of Asian immigration was well ahead of public opinion, particularly in suburbs and workplaces. I don't know what research and population data he found, and where he found it, which enabled him to reach that conclusion.

Blainey's comments were published in *The Age* on 20 March 1984, and attracted a lot of letters to the editor.

One response from a Vietnamese migrant is worth thinking about:

> We came here with nothing and started a new life, like many Italians and Greeks did. The second and third generation Italians and Greeks now live normal lives, just like normal Australians. Maybe my grandchildren will be like that.

That Vietnamese grandfather sounds a lot like the European migrants after World War II.

Apart from the obvious racial perspective, the idea that Australia is down under at the end of the world is meaningless. The old concept was an English perception. It may have been true when measured by ship speed in miles and time. The voyage by sea took six weeks. The trip now takes 20 hours by air.

The centre of world trade has moved from Europe and the United States to Asia. US and European exporters were much larger suppliers for Australia in the past, but (from the present perspective of our new and much faster supply chains) are further away than the factories of China, Korea, Thailand, Vietnam, and Malaysia. These factories also derive logistics efficiencies from the freight *entrepots* of Singapore and Hong Kong, which have huge harbours working 24/7 and shipping connections to the rest of the world.

Finally, Brisbane and Port Botany harbours are our closest to Asia, if you ignore the claims of Darwin. That city lacks a lot of the necessary infrastructure and domestic demand conditions for a major port (including lacking at least one major proximate domestic market). Both ports are now either totally owned (in the case of Brisbane) or partially owned (the third terminal at Port Botany) by Hutchison Whampoa and the United Arab Emirates. The latter also bought the ports of Newcastle and Port Kembla.

The Port of Melbourne is also in the process of being sold, as a 50-year lease, and it would not be surprising if one of the two global port operators already operating on the Australian east coast wanted to buy Melbourne's port to create economies in the supply chain and keep their major competitor out of that chain.

I wonder if Professor Blainey still thinks that Britain is home. In 2016 he is obviously wrong. Less obviously, our connection with the US is weakening. From the perspective of trade and personal ties, Britain might as well be on the other side of the moon. US ownership in Australia and its military presence in Darwin remain significant, but we are not an American outpost. Still, much of our military alliance remains. The Battle of the Coral Sea happened 70 years ago, and some people do not forget the indifferent treatment of Australian troops by US General Douglas Macarthur in New Guinea. Nevertheless, we have been strong supporters and allies of the US in every foreign conflict since then.

The Department of Immigration and Border Protection (which now includes Customs) states that the purpose of immigration is to build the economy, shape society, support the labour market, and reunite families. That is a big social step forward for Australia since the infamous dictation test that Customs used until the 1950s to keep migrants out of Australia when it didn't like their colour or look. We had our own version of apartheid in those days.

In the 2011 Australian census, 27 per cent of respondents were born overseas. Their major places of birth were Britain (5.3 per cent); New Zealand (2.5 per cent); China (1.8 per cent); India (1.3 per cent); Vietnam (0.9 per cent); and Italy (0.9 per cent).

Chinese students comprise 23 per cent of international student enrolments. They have temporary visas. They eat and drink, pay rent, buy consumer durables, go to the movies, and use public transport. They often have part-time jobs in hospitality, or pack shelves at 4.00 a.m. at Woolworths and Coles. They live in student quarters and cheap housing in or close to our universities and colleges of advanced education.

The British and New Zealand share of the Australian population is shrinking, but we have not been overrun by anyone else. A lot of students from other Asian countries besides China come to Australia. Like the Chinese, most of them (or their parents) are paying fees, working part time, and buying goods and services. They may stay, but most will return to their home countries. They are a wonderful, temporary cultural addition to our society. They haven't been traumatised by a world war the way our last major influx of migrants was (although their parents were). They have had an opportunity to receive an education that their parents and grandparents never had.

The Chinese first came to Australia for the gold rushes in Victoria. Most went back to China when it was over. A lot of the gold they found went with them. The first migrants after the British were the Lebanese. They came to Australia in the late nineteenth century. They were Catholics, and became resourceful traders selling direct to farm households.

From the beginning of the 1950s, migrants from Europe came to Australia from the German and European prisoner-of-war and extermination camps that were simply left abandoned after the defeat of the Axis powers and the occupation of Berlin. English migrants came in the 1950s — the 'Ten-Pound Poms'. Arthur Calwell, Gough Whitlam's predecessor as leader of the Australian Labor Party, and a minister in the last Labor government before Bob Menzies became prime minister, introduced the post-war 'work for citizenship' program to develop major regional dams and the Snowy Mountain Scheme.

In 1946, the first European migrants left behind a Europe impoverished and devastated by a very expensive war in both lives lost and money wasted. The European economies had gone backwards. They had lost a lot of their assets in the US and South Africa.

However, basing the impact of the arrival of European migrants on Calwell's migration initiative is not strictly accurate. We received a singular and substantial infusion of entrepreneurial talent and intellectual brilliance when the *Dunera* prison ship arrived in Australia with over 2,000 young Jewish men who had been shipped out of Britain in 1941 after the fall of Dunkirk. This was a piece of British government and general hysteria following that horrendous debacle. It was widely believed that invasion was imminent, and anyone of German or Austrian birth was suspected of being either a spy or a saboteur.

Those boys (many were still in their teens or early twenties) had the intellect, energy, and drive to escape from an ascendant regime in Germany that would have murdered them in death camps. The *Dunera* boys contributed greatly to Australia's intellectual, social, and economic development for the next 50 years and more. My great mentor and friend for many years, Ernest Rodeck, and his partner, Fred Lowen, were typical *Dunera* boys. Their creation, Fler furniture, is still a sought-after Australian brand for class, comfort, and design. People still want to buy Fler products, 60 years after they were first made.

Some of the British migrants in the early 1950s were soon back in uniform as Customs officers and prison guards. Those who went to Customs were often clever achievers who lacked the education that would have allowed them to enter the clerical division of the Australian Public Service.

The Australian Leaving Certificate (which students sat for after five years of secondary school education, when most had turned 17) was a basic qualification for entry into the Third Division of the Commonwealth Public Service, as it was called then. In the

1960s most young people left school when they were 15 after the Intermediate Certificate. In the 1930s they left when they were 12 after the completion of what was called the Primary Final. My father began work when he was 12 years old.

The Fourth Division Preventive Officers searched ships, looked at passports, and opened passengers' baggage. They confiscated alcohol, cheeses, and other foodstuffs. They didn't look for drugs. Opium was the only drug at the time, and it was the drug of choice of sailors, not passengers. Customs searched ships for opium. Times have changed since then.

There were a lot fewer travellers, but they were examined more closely (and physically) than they are today. Virtually all passengers arrived after a six-week trip from the UK, including passage through the Suez Canal. A lot of the processes were prejudiced and influenced by the so-called White Australia Policy.

There were Italians, Germans, Greeks, and other Europeans. We used to call the latter White Russians, as they often came from countries that had been part of Russia. That name dates back to the Russian Civil War during and after World War I, when the Whites (supporters of the Czar) fought the Reds — the Bolshevik communists. Many of the old White Russians and Ukrainians had been held in German and Soviet prisoner-of-war camps. They were lucky to be alive. Stalin had a long memory, and some Ukrainians had been prison guards in the German death camps.

The Australian government's migration scheme that paid the migrants' fare by ship required them to work on location to build dams, the Snowy Mountain Scheme, and other great pieces of Australian infrastructure. The hiatus until they could live normally again often involved a full two years of cold loneliness in the Snowy Mountains camps for men only. They went to town at Jindabyne once a week. Once the migrants were established and could find a place to live, they sent for their families.

The European refugees released from German and Russian camps after the war eventually settled in the outer-western suburbs of Sydney, in country New South Wales, and in Melbourne. They generally had no homes or close families to go back to in Europe.

In the early 1950s, the number of Greeks living in Melbourne was said to be surpassed only by the population of Athens. Nearly every milk bar/restaurant in country and suburban New South Wales in the 1950s was once owned by Greek migrants from the island of Kythera. They lived in, and ate meals from the food sold in their shops. The home living space was out the back of the milk bar, but the kitchen was in the front.

Some milk bars had ambitious menus for the time, and could produce an edible steak. Australian cuisine hadn't advanced far by the early 1940s. The Paragon milk bar in the Blue Mountains was famous for its cuisine, which was basically steak, onions, tomato sauce, eggs, and chips. Over the years, Greek migrants often bought a small piece of land at every opportunity. Their willingness to work long hours, combined with their amiable natures, cleverness, and financial nous were the foundations of their fortunes.

The Italian migrants were equally industrious. They were committed to their extended families. If there were four brothers, they would save together to buy a house for the eldest brother, then they saved together for a house for the next eldest. There was no sibling rivalry.

By the 1970s, some of the migrants were able to pay private-school fees for their children (often $30,000 per child a year) and send them to university. In the early 1960s — before Gough Whitlam's largesse (of a first degree paid for by the government) — university fees were equal to a year's average wages.

One famous story of Greek hospitality during World

War II (which I believe to be true) involved the Paragon milk bar at Gundagai in country New South Wales, about 300 kilometres from Sydney. Australian prime minister Ben Chifley was being driven through Gundagai on Sunday night at close to midnight, returning to Melbourne. There weren't many (or any) commercial airplane services in those days, and none on Sundays near midnight. The PM and his staff and driver had not eaten, so they knocked on the Paragon's closed door (there were a lot of milk bars called the Paragon in New South Wales and Victoria). The proprietor got them a steak dinner. The PM asked what he could do for the Greek proprietor, who had left his bed to cook the steaks. He asked the PM for a federal government tea quota, which was duly provided. That was worth more than money in 1944.

For the next 60 years and more than two generations, many of those European migrants — Jewish, Italian, and Greek, and other Eastern European refugees from the camps after World War II — were family creators and benefactors, providing expensive cars, trips to Europe, and very expensive homes for their wives, children, and grandchildren. They had known hardship, but their grandchildren never did.

Sometimes the children and grandchildren did not want to know their migrant forebears. They were upwardly socially mobile, and a bit ashamed of their forebears. In the mid-1960s, I heard one girl chastising her father for answering the phone when I called. She had instructed him not to answer the phone at the time her University of Sydney friends were likely to be calling. She didn't want her friends to hear her father's thick European accent. (This doesn't seem to be a common event with Chinese and Vietnamese migrants today. They are often directly involved in their parents' and grandparents' retail and wholesale activities.) He had earned a substantial fortune as a market stall-owner in the hurly-burly of

Sydney's produce markets. They lived in a good house in Double Bay, an exclusive suburb of Sydney. Today, those houses are worth millions of dollars. His daughter wore the most beautiful clothes I had ever seen at that stage of my life. Like many students at Sydney University in the mid-1960s, she got rid of her European accent or had already lost it at an eastern-suburban private school.

First-year Arts used to be called Marriage One. Many of the North Shore and eastern-suburbs girls had already found a medical student or a likely lawyer to marry by the end of the year. The girl I mentioned married a lawyer (whose father was Greek). He became the senior partner of a mid-sized legal practice in central Sydney.

In the early and mid-1950s, European migrants often worked 12 hours or more a day, seven days a week, as proprietors of fruit shops and milk bars. Their children often lived by eating the stale stock and overcooked hamburgers and chips left at the end of the day or the week. The children worked in the milk bar or fruit shop when they came home from school. The father always had a big bundle of cash in his pocket. I doubt the taxman saw much of it.

The Asian migrants have now followed this pathway to prosperity, and have extended the milk-bar and fruit-shop strategy to include an enormous number of restaurants in Sydney and Melbourne. The first wave came in the 1970s with South Vietnamese refugees. They were no longer welcome in the Vietnam ruled by the victorious North. Some went to Hong Kong for years, but eventually found their way to Australia. It was a migration that often resulted in the survival of the fittest and the smartest and most industrious.

I met one woman who was a senior public servant in the Immigration Department. She was in her forties, and was the only survivor of a family of 10 children who had travelled by open boat with their parents from Vietnam to Hong Kong, and stayed there for six years. They had been robbed at sea by pirates who took everything they possessed.

Asian entrepreneurs have dominated the clothing and footwear industries in Australia since the major companies in the industry were sold off in the early 1990s after clothing and footwear quotas were discontinued by Paul Keating.

The little pieces of property they acquired, and the skills, knowledge, and work ethic the Greek and Italian migrants brought with them were the foundations of their fortunes. They were also great networkers with migrants from their own country or even from the same village. But their fundamental asset was their own industry, intelligence, and willingness to 'have a go'.

The Asian immigrants from China, Vietnam, and Thailand in the past 40 years (and the Catholic Lebanese for nearly 80 years before them) have followed the same formula for success by their effort, intelligence, habitual saving, and long hours of work.

The European, Asian, and American founders of multinational corporations were not a new breed of entrepreneurs: their small-business models and their tax strategies were simply a variation on what had been a standard business philosophy for hundreds or even thousands of years.

That philosophy has two parts. The first part is: 'Buy cheap, charge dear, and don't pay any tax. Use cheap labour (particularly your children and relatives). Employ people who work for very little money and don't complain about working conditions. Feed them out of the shop.'

The second part is: 'Jack is as good as his master'.

Dunera boys Ernest Rodeck and Fred Lowen were the founders of Fler Furniture (which they started in a disused brothel, where they had to bar the door late at night from uninformed and inebriated previous customers). Ernest told me that the common-man philosophy was the reason he settled in Australia, rather than staying with his mother, father, and sister in New York. They had settled in America after fleeing the Nazis after the German annexation of Austria in 1938. There is no doubt that people of outstanding ability and personal qualities could and did overcome the class barriers in the Australia of 1945.

They couldn't do that in Britiain before 1945. Britain was still highly class conscious up until 1939. It had lost a generation of fine young men in the trenches in World War I, and another on the battlefields of World War II, the young men who had been born to be the next generation of its leaders. Moreover, after World War II, the propertied classes were impoverished by the tax system and by the loans and costs incurred by the war.

In the twenty-first century, places like Hong Kong, Singapore, and the United Arab Emirates provide the best opportunities for industrious and clever young people to work and earn an income that enables them to aspire to the middle-class home and lifestyle that their parents had. Much of these places' advantages arise from their tax concessions.

In the Arab states, the older generation that created the oil-rich economies is experiencing the 'aristocracy disease'. Their grandchildren do not work, and are hugely conspicuous consumers. Generally, the world seems to be moving back towards class-based societies. They are plutocracies that are partially (but substantially) based on birth.

CHAPTER FIFTEEN

Reinventing Australia

Possibly the major innovation of the twenty-first century (apart from the internet) is the multinational technology model for the supply chain. Its global reach and speed to market through the interaction of multiple delivery processes was made possible by technological innovations such as the internet, television, side-loading and back-loading container trucks, mobile phones, air-conditioning, and 24/7 ports, depots, and supermarkets.

This model is very efficient, but is not affordable for small or even medium-sized import/export market participants. It has been a major reason for their decline. They simply cannot compete. Personal service is appreciated, but consumers want to pay less and buy everything in one place.

The disparate innovations (in freight, clearance, storage, break-bulk, container delivery to customers, and return-to-container depots) made for great improvements in the supply chain. The innovations that, generally, came at about the same time, had much more power combined than any single invention or improved process. Transport-cost reductions, government barrier simplification, duty reductions, and other barrier innovations created a quantum shift in the speed of both the air and sea supply chains, and created huge reductions in the time it took to get goods to market. Importers became very aware of the cost and time savings created by these logistics advantages. The changes meant that they were out of their money (which might have been funded by an overdraft) for much less time.

Some retail practices developed today illustrate the huge shift in speed. Woolworths and Coles, for example, put their day receipts on the overnight cash market. They don't put the cash into the bank, but they don't waste even a day of financial returns. They just tell their banks how much they received from customers in the day at all their retail outlets, and the banks put that amount on the short-term overnight money market. It is in the banks' interests to trust their biggest customers.

The point is that it would be impossible to count the money and card deposits from over 2,000 retail outlets in the 12 hours available. Present shopping and stocking hours wouldn't even allow that much time. The major retailers are getting close to 24/7 operations, even if the stores aren't open all the time. Cleaning up and restocking when the doors are closed is part of their day.

The only anachronism is the customs entry system. The imports clearance system has not changed since the early 1960s. Although it has been computerised, and the entries are passed in milliseconds, there has to be an entry for each and every shipment. Customs brokers prepare those, and they don't work 24/7. Neither does Customs. The same goods for the same importer may have to be classified and entered individually thousands of times a year.

The individual customs entry system was challenged by the Australian Exporters and Importers Group (which included Coles and Woolworths) that I set up in the late 1990s. Legislation for periodic entry (that is, monthly or weekly entries) passed through parliament in 2000, and it received royal assent in the early 2000s.

However, the change was rescinded after computer glitches between the customs system and the stevedoring operators caused a month's delay in cargo delivery over the months just before and after Christmas 2005.

The delay affected importers and retailers over the Christmas period, and they ultimately received about $800 million in compensation payments from the government (Christmas trees and decorations are not marketable in late January) to compensate for overtime payments for wharf storage to the stevedores and loss of income. The chief executive of Customs (Lionel Woodward) retired early.

The obvious question is why this efficiency hasn't been tried again. In 2016, importers and their brokers still have to lodge a separate entry for every shipment, even though the same goods may be entered five times a day by the same company from the same supplier, and no matter how many times they have entered the same imported goods before for any number of years. That also applies for GST due on individual shipments.

The irony perhaps is that the only importers who are able to lodge weekly settlement entries are those who deal in tobacco and alcohol — commodities that attract high duties on account of their status as of doubtful social utility. This is because the duty is the equivalent of the excise, and is much more than the customs value for spirits and tobacco products.

Conclusion

This book is essentially about how multinational corporations have kept most of their income for the past 25 years, or even longer. The primary element in their strategy is to delay finalisation of their tax position as long as possible and minimise any ultimate transfer-pricing settlements with tax authorities. That gives them the use of the money (in some cases for more than a decade) they ultimately have to pay to the authorities, or they don't pay anything because they have accumulated losses. The second element is simply not to pay tax at all by use of a variety of tax tricks and tax havens supported by some national governments.

Through the use of these strategies the multinationals also improve their bargaining position with governments that are hungry for multimillion-dollar audit settlements they had not factored into their budgets. There is an element of a windfall gain from multinational settlements for government treasuries. They will generally settle for payment of a lot less than the amount that is actually overdue.

The Australian taxation environment provides several examples of particular tax benefits for companies involved in what is known as base erosion and profit shifting (BEPS). First, the companies are usually able to negotiate a tax result, including penalties and late-payment interest, that is less than the tax amount they actually owe. And in the meantime they have had the use of those tax-due funds for years.

Second, multinational affiliates that were manufacturers but have left Australia and are now marketer-distributors are also generally able to keep their tax losses when they leave Australia or change their business from manufacturers to marketer-distributors. This has happened with motor-vehicle manufacturers that have already transitioned to marketer-distributers. It also happened with main street major retailers of luxury goods that moved offshore and now focus on internet trading. Virtually all substantial brand-name owners have transitioned to marketer-distributors on the internet in the past 10 years. Internet sales of their products are part of the reason. They don't need a shopfront anymore, particularly if their products aren't apparel or shoes. They sometimes retain shops in capital cities as flagship stores.

Technology advances that have created and enabled the internet are the essential innovations that underpin the BEPS threat to the world economy. It is the practical computer system that enables the BEPS strategy to work. Otherwise, accountants would still be sneaking furtively off to Switzerland with bags full of money. Now all that is necessary is a bank transfer. Sometimes there are lots of bank transfers to different countries to confuse the money trail.

The multinational strategy has been to test a new market's response by entering it by way of arm's-length distributors. Next, the parent company establishes manufacturing subsidiaries in the new market that operate behind tariff and quota walls. Once the multinational's brand name has won sufficient consumer awareness in the market, it is time for BEPS and the shift to low-cost manufacturing in an Asian country that does not tax foreign-sourced income. The tactic depends on the value of the brand name and the after-sales structure in the new market. The distributors are thanked and terminated. They cannot do much about it because they do not have manufacturing knowhow and do not own the brand name.

Quality-control manufacturing was a great productive step forward, but it put a lot of people in higher-income economies out of work.

Additionally, imports are generally no longer subject to quotas or duty rates above 5 per cent. Most goods are dutiable at zero or 3 per cent. They are not subject to non-tariff barriers, and do not compete with local manufacturers except in Japan, China, Korea, and the United States. Those places are the home countries of most of the world's multinationals.

It was inevitable that BEPS would occur. The tax-avoidance or reduction strategy thrives in an environment where import barriers are low or non-existent. The technique is to use BEPS and pay little or no tax in environments where duty rates are much lower than the company tax rate. Increasing the customs value of imported products is a simple way to repatriate profits and leave the affiliate in perpetual tax losses. That is the situation in Australia. The imports price is inflated by an overseas affiliate, and the local subsidiary makes a loss and so pays no company tax.

There may be no actual payment of funds in the transaction between the subsidiary and the parent. The plus-and-minus outcomes are recorded and netted off in the accounts, but there is no necessity to pay any of the outstanding amounts. No one outside the tax haven (which may be Switzerland or Liechtenstein, or some other place that is difficult for other national tax authorities to access) has any idea how much money is owed by subsidiaries to other subsidiaries or head offices.

Accounting balances are maintained between the parent company and their affiliates all over the world. They may only be brought to account if there is a particular financial or market-reporting requirement at some future time to bolster the bottom line and support a new acquisition or an unpopular distribution of dividends.

Australian consumers have shown no resentment about or resistance to the departure of ownership of major brands that had previously been manufactured in Australia. Some of these brands may retain some sales on account of being sentimental favourites, or because purchasers don't even know that they are no longer Australian-owned. Some clothing brands meeting this principle have been promoted by Australian sporting champions.

We are too far away from major markets other than China, Japan, and Korea to sell Australian retail products unless they have a fashion or upmarket niche.

Asian countries look after their manufacturers through a variety of measures that are often not publicly known. They are happy to buy our commodities and raw materials, to which they can add value. However, they maintain non-tariff barriers where they have politically powerful domestic manufacturers. Some European countries also continue to maintain non-tariff barriers.

With the ending of border protection through duties and tariffs, company and income taxes are paid by local companies but not by multinationals. Transfer pricing is why. For 25 years it has been destroying the national tax bases that provide the revenue to fund the social responsibilities of governments to their people. Moreover, the Big Four accountants use devices and techniques that ensure that the resolution of tax audits is complex, glacially slow, and confusing. All this has to stop, or the global economy will be damaged irrevocably.

Postscript

Change is the only eternal constant for the human race. The history of humanity on our planet is a history of continuous population movements. Sometimes people settle without disruptive interference between the original inhabitants and the migrant waves. Aboriginal Australians did so, for tens of thousands of years. It helps if you have a huge island continent remote from other major land masses, where the population of the island is small and scattered, and there is a culture of following the available food as the seasons change. They were superbly adapted to an environment that was basically closed from the rest of the world by the sheer distance that had to be travelled to reach a place which, for eighteenth-century economies, had nothing of apparent substance to offer.

Ultimately, Britain (the great power of the nineteenth century, after the defeat and exile of Napoleon) began to seek a remote place to imprison convicts at the lowest possible cost and least risk to the British government. Virtually all the convicts were originally sentenced to hang, but keeping and watching them until that event cost money. The solution was to send them as far away as possible at a negligible cost. The distance, the impenetrable hinterland, and the virtual impossibility of finding a way back to Britain seemed to create a collection of barriers that meant being sentenced 'for the term of your natural life' was literally the case. Very few managed to make it back to Britain, and the punishment for those few who did and were caught was the death penalty.

Aboriginal Australians were not like the Incas and Mayas. They did not mine gold or silver. Their ornamentation came from the colours of earth sands. Their religious beliefs were recorded in their rock carvings and in bark paintings. They followed their food, and lived on the land in open camps. There were no temples filled with precious things. Even the graves of the dead were left in the trees or at camps that had been abandoned in the tribe's constant movement to the next source of food, leaving behind a place where they believed the spirits of the dead dwelt. That was not indifference or ignorance: its real purpose was to avoid plagues and diseases.

Over 30 years, Australia changed from a prison settlement in Sydney Cove close to the sea, to farms located as far out as Parramatta. Its rural history has been described and discussed in many books and articles. It is sufficient to say that Australia rode on the sheep's back until the discovery of gold. Now we rely on wheat fields and mining pits.

The history of the Aboriginal Australians has been discussed by many authors. It is mentioned here simply as a matter of respect. They were the first Australians — the first migrants, who arrived 40,000 years ago. There was no one here, so they were the original owners of Australia. They didn't have to plant a flag, as the Europeans did when they first came to a country.

Other migrants have arrived following wars and the discovery of gold, into the perfect climate for growing wool and wheat, and a land prolific in minerals for the mining. Australia has always ridden on the back of some resource. Each wave of migrants has brought with it elements of its original culture, and, as with Britain, sometimes previous cultures have resisted the changes. Resistance to change in Australian society has always existed. We are no different in that respect from the rest of the world. Strangers with different ways of life and religious beliefs are viewed with suspicion.

Every so often, the world is struck by a major plague or calamity. Meteors have hit Earth and may have precipitated an ice age. The Black Death wiped out a quarter of the population of Europe. The Hundred Years War in Germany killed a third of the population. The potato famine did the same in Ireland; it was the cause of the great Irish migration to the United States and Australia in the nineteenth century, to such an extent that the population of Ireland declined in the second half of the nineteenth century.

There has been global financial fraud and misrepresentation before. It certainly happened on the stock exchange in England and Holland in the seventeenth century, and on the US stock exchange in 1930. The global financial crisis of 2007 was a misnomer. It was actually the global financial fraud, perpetrated by greedy Wall Street smarties. The acronym NINJA has probably been forgotten by most of us. The NINJAs were the hundreds of thousands of Americans lent money that they could never repay to buy houses. They had 'no income, no job, and no assets'.

In the financial history of the world there has never been as destructive a financial blight on global economies as transfer pricing. Yet Weimar Germany's inflation in the 1920s destroyed the middle class of one country. That led to World War II. Some speculators became very rich during the hyperinflation.

It's a lot like John Wyndham's *The Trouble with Lichen*. Lower taxes and a shorter supply chain for perfect-quality brand-name products seems a desirable goal. Yet what looked to be a logistics and quality boon for mankind in the first years of the twenty-first century has become a curse. We are losing control of the world economy to the relatively small group of plutocrats who own the brand names. Their accountants have created a tax-avoidance machine that makes so much money and pays so little tax that the machine will ultimately destroy governments and nations unless it is stopped. It is not a matter of courtesy. Stopping it is a global necessity. The welfare of the old, the very young, the uneducated, and the helpless depends upon its being stopped.

The alarm exhibited by the OECD, the G9, and the G20 is unparalleled in the history of those international organisations. They include virtually all the major nations of the world within their memberships. There has never been an avoidance strategy that has involved anything like the amount of money expropriated from the global taxation base by the multinationals and their accounting advisers through transfer-pricing strategies.

My transfer-pricing experience dates back 30 years to what was the global beginning of the problem. There had been a few isolated court cases before then, back as far as 1945, but that was before the concerted attack on international tax collections in subsidiary locations by virtually all multinationals.

The developed nations of the world have created a mechanism through taxation that has allowed them to build schools, hospitals, aged facilities, roads, and all the infrastructure that makes living in an industrial economy worthwhile. Now multinational corporations are threatening those fundamental goods.

The companies and their Big Four advisers may not think about what they are doing. But they are too clever not to comprehend the global damage they are causing. They have been able to avoid many trillions of dollars of tax in the past 25 years through transfer pricing. There has been no end to their appetite for tax-free money.

Why do some people want to be so rich? They can be rich within the existing tax regimes, but they have an insatiable appetite for more. Some people, regardless, just want more.

Appendices

APPENDIX A

The golden age of tax planning

Much of this appendix makes use of a paper written in the early 1990s by an eminent UK Queen's Counsel, David Goldbloom.

Goldbloom, a senior QC of more than 25 years standing at London's Grays Inn tax chambers, wrote a paper titled, 'The Golden Age of Tax Planning'. His discussion of tax schemes dates back to World War I and the debates in the UK parliament. It deals with the early days of tax planning. It is an important source because of its clear exposition and quotation of the decisions given by several UK Law Lords over decades.

Much of the logic expressed by the Lords provides a relevant structure for the arguments and logic that clear-thinking judges can apply to transfer-pricing cases that reach the courts in 2016 and beyond. In the two Australian cases, a total of nine judges' logic has been dismissive of the transactional net margin method (TNMM), and it is likely that future Australian courts will follow that logic.

The golden age of tax planning has been in progress globally for the past 25 years. At least, a golden age is what it has been for the Big Four accountancy firms and their clients. The globalisation of the multinational affiliates into one tax and pricing strategy directly managed by the parent company rather than a strategy for every national market initiated a process of tax avoidance that has become a major problem for governments that need to tax companies to generate revenue.

Taxing wealthy individuals is increasingly difficult. As we live longer, are at school longer, and are retired longer, the cost to the state for pensions, hospitals, retirement homes, child assistance for working mothers, and Medicare is growing and putting ever-greater pressure on the tax base. More bad news for governments is that the company tax base is being eroded severely by the concentration of market supply in the hands of a relatively few global corporations. In some market niches there are now only one or two retailers where there used to be 10. Internet trading will, in the case of Australia, probably exacerbate that trend over the next 10 years.

Richard Goyder, the chief executive of Wesfarmers (the owner of Coles and Bunnings), commented in an address to the National Press Club on 5 August 2014 that Wesfarmers paid $1.5 billion in tax in 2013–14 while Aldi and Costco paid nothing. Why should that be so? The answer is that transfer pricing by multinationals has created a market and profit advantage for them that, ultimately, will destroy their competitors. Coles, along with Woolworths, is one of the largest employers in Australia. Most of its hundreds of thousands of employees are women trying to earn enough money working part time to keep the family afloat.

There have only been two recent cases in Australia regarding transfer pricing. In both cases, the methodology under review was the multinationals' methodology of choice. The cases (including an appeal in one case to a full bench of the Federal Court by the tax commissioner, arguing for the TNMM) were lost on the basis that it was not an appropriate way to arrive at the arm's-length price of the goods and services being considered. Yet that is the method used by over 90 per cent of multinationals. The obvious conclusion is that the TNMM suits their purposes (and sometimes the purposes of the tax commissioner) best.

It is a pity that former High Court Chief Justice Gleeson believed that the court was not the place to hear tax cases, because the tax cases that would reach the High Court involve a lot of money, and offer substantial precedents for future behaviour. It is important to establish foundation principles for issues of import for the Australian economy. Some of these issues involve money that was intended by legislators to be paid in tax. Multinationals not paying a fair share of tax is a core social problem for the people of Australia and the rest of the world. Perhaps with a new chief justice, and as generational change among the higher judiciary occurs (combined with the social costs of transfer pricing), there may be a change in attitude. The Chevron case may portend such a change.

The fact that the ATO has taken the action against Chevron is significant. The ATO won the first hearing of the case, which could have been stillborn if the judge had ruled against the ATO. It is now likely that Chevron will appeal and that at least six years will be consumed with hearings (with further appeals by the loser) and passage through other courts and appeals before the plaintiff can even seek leave to appeal to the High Court.

The House of Lords has been hearing tax cases in Britain for one hundred years or more. In that time there has developed a magnificent volume of precedents and opinions that provide an invaluable perspective on transfer pricing and other taxation schemes.

David Goldbloom, in the aforementioned paper, quotes then British prime minister Lloyd George as saying: 'It is perfectly true that you can make legal arrangements ... to evade tax ... the moment it is done the Inland Revenue will stop all that kind of spider web ... The only reason it was not done was because I was informed that at the present time it was not worthwhile.'

It is certainly worthwhile now for economies to unravel the artificial schemes and devices that have been so remorselessly employed by the multinationals and their global tax advisers, the Big Four accounting firms.

Goldbloom quotes Lord Tomlin in the Duke of Windsor's case as saying: 'Every man is entitled to order his affairs so that the tax attaching under the appropriate acts is less than it would otherwise be.'

I suppose company affairs can be ordered, in the context of the words of the existing legislation (which in Australia dates back to 1934) so as to pay no tax at all. That seems to be the case at present for internet-based companies without a permanent residence in a taxing jurisdiction, and for multinationals performing their circuitous brolga dance. That is why tax laws should be amended and senior tax officers should seek retrospective amendments, just as Deputy Commissioner Mark Konza is doing in the Chevron case.

Clearly, in many legal circumstances, retrospective laws are against the common interest. Yet we are not talking about criminal law or other laws relating to human behaviour. We are talking about a deliberate and broad-based assault by multinationals upon national tax collections, combined with their growing control of national markets for goods and services. If this strategy continues unchecked, it will ultimate destroy the foundations of the global industrial society while enriching a very small percentage of the population.

Taxation is not supposed to be a game between those

protecting the revenue of the state and those seeking, either to evade tax (with the possibility of a jail sentence) or avoid it (with the possibility of substantial penalties). It is too important to the national communities for that.

Goldbloom wrote that there had been only four cases involving tax-avoidance principles until 1971. That was when asset stripping began, where schemes were tailored to a client's individual circumstances. Goldbloom wrote: '[A]nd to begin with, it all worked ... Revenue accepted the schemes and tax was saved; and, I suppose, the Exchequer suffered or, at any rate was perceived to suffer.'

Goldbloom wrote that this golden age for planners didn't last very long. A test case was taken to the House of Lords. Goldbloom's paper was written in the early 1990s, when the impending torrent of transfer pricing was just a trickle.

He wrote: '[T]here has been a cataract of cases since 1971 and I presume there is now a genuine distaste for tax avoidance', and 'the Tax Lords were initially attracted by sheer cleverness then repulsed by the extent to which they are used'. If that's the feeling at the beginning of transfer pricing, the negative attitude of the Law Lords and many other judges all over the world now can only be imagined.

Goldbloom quotes Lord Scarman as saying in 1984:

> I am aware, and the legal profession (and others) must understand that the law in this area is in an early stage of development ... I am concerned more to chart a way between principles accepted and not to be rejected than to attempt anything so ambitious as to determine finally the safe channel of acceptable tax-avoidance shelves into the dangerous channels of unacceptable tax evasion.

The law has not developed as it should have, because tax authorities and governments in general have not been prepared to tackle the increasingly predatory tax strategies and artificial arrangements the multinationals have adopted.

Lord Scarman also predicted that the law would develop from case to case. This is happening in Australia, as the courts have rejected the TNMM regardless of whether it was being promoted by the taxpayer or the tax commissioner.

In 1921, in *Cape Brandy Syndicate v Inland Revenue Commissioners (12TC 358 at 366)*, Justice Rowlett enunciated a clear set of tax principles, saying:

> In a taxing statute one has to look merely at what is clearly said. There is no room for any intendment. There is no equity about a tax. There is no presumption as to a tax. Nothing is to be read in, nothing is to be implied. One can look fairly at the language used.

Goldbloom concludes: 'I believe that the presumption, perhaps of everybody including the politicians, is tax has become part of the law of nature. Perhaps it is no longer right to say that man is born free; man is born to be taxed but occasionally has liberties.'

His analytical view is precise and correct, even if it seems to manifest an element of wistfulness at the outcome. If you are fortunate enough to be born into a society that has police, hospitals, roads, schools, free medical and dental care for the poor, old-age homes and pensions, then you are born into a society where you are expected to pay your fair share of tax according to your means. You may not appreciate fully that our civilised societies are built upon the generosity of those who are well off passing, without complaint or devious means of avoidance, some of their prosperity to those less fortunate via the state mechanism of tax.

The Scrooge multinationals who want to pay no taxes at all should be told there are still prisons and poor houses, though those who must go there are excused the indignity and hunger of the Dickensian workhouses. In Australia, at least, the state pays for the social services and pension safety net, and provides some foundation level of dignity to the old, the sick, the defenceless, and the weak. Not many countries behave in the same way.

The ATO has been substantially involved in transfer-pricing reviews, audits, advance-pricing arrangements, and other tax-review products for more than 25 years. It seeks fairly simple, initial levels of participation in the processes from multinational affiliates in Australia. The ATO is aware that parent companies and regional offices have been managing the transfer-pricing issue on a worldwide basis for decades. Yet initial probes by the ATO often result in an Australian subsidiary client producing documentation that is out of date, does not represent the present functions, assets, and risks of the affiliate, and does not indicate any awareness of the Australian rulings and legislation.

The taxpayer documentation review and negotiation process is like watching cold oil drip. No one in Australia will take responsibility for documentation, and no one will make much effort to explain how and why a company's functions, assets and risks paradigm have altered during decades of product change, divestment of subsidiaries, acquisitions of new business, the impact of new government policies, or any other change that may impact upon the transfer-pricing analysis. Often the documentation is badly out of date and does not accurately represent the subsidiary's functions, assets, and risks at the time of the audit — and certainly not at the time of judicial review.

For smaller Australian multinational affiliates, the entire issue is outside their control, beyond their budget, and not in their interest. The managing director of a major company recently told me that transfer pricing 'was not part of his remit'. I think he felt that he would be poorly regarded if he brought the issue up with his European head office. I know that whenever a matter blows up, the global transfer-pricing people from the United States and Asia come to Australia for the discussion with the ATO. This would obviously be the case for European multinationals as well. Local executives generally have a minor role, and cannot make final settlement decisions.

Regional offices (not to speak of head offices) are loath to focus and spend money on what is a relatively small market in the context of the global (or even the Asian-region) business, unless there is a threat. Then they pay attention.

To some extent, that attitude explains why Australian transfer-pricing reviews are not an integral part of the multinational global audit approach. It costs too much in time and money. In the early years of transfer pricing the Australian subsidiary often got only a paragraph or two in the hundreds of pages of transfer-pricing manuals for all subsidiaries of a major multinational trading in over 200 national markets.

It is a shame that there have been only two cases in the past 25 years that have begun to create a judicial attitude towards the appropriate arm's-length methodology for multinational affiliates operating in Australia. The development of a history of case law will be an invaluable cost efficiency for both multinationals and the ATO.

When undertaking the task of creating transfer-pricing documentation (and having the expectation that the ATO will eventually review it), there is an obvious temptation to use the easy, self-serving TNMM method, especially if a comparables database can be employed that fits the company's predetermined global transfer-pricing position.

There is little doubt that most multinationals with many subsidiaries (some have more than two hundred) would want to manage and standardise the chaos and contradictions of using different methodologies and taxation principles in different countries. Using one simple method for all subsidiaries based on external data sources is the easy way out, even if it was incorrect originally and falls into greater error as the functions, assets, and risks of the affiliate in that country change over time.

Nonetheless, the law of large numbers would suggest that some multinationals would use different transfer-pricing methods in different countries. For example, they might be marketer-distributers in large countries, and manufacturers in smaller countries. Financial and exchange-management losses and gains might be centralised in one affiliate acting globally; and technology developments might be centrally located somewhere else. Finally, for countries where there are significant competitors, there might be other strategic reasons for methodological differentiation.

So, the list of reasons for individual affiliates' functions, assets, and risks differing from country to country is lengthy. Not all multinational subsidiaries are the same; and the market and taxation environments where they are located are certainly not all the same. One size does not fit all global transfer-pricing documentation for a multinational.

APPENDIX B

Recent Australian court cases

Roche Pharmaceuticals (2008)

Roche Pharmaceuticals Australia is a subsidiary of a Swiss parent company that used the comparable uncontrolled price (CUP) method to arrive at prices charged internally among the parent and its subsidiaries. The ATO argued that the TNMM was the appropriate method and that, on this basis, the company owed the ATO many millions of dollars. Justice Garry Downes, the president of the Administrative Appeals Tribunal, came down in favour of CUPs, and was critical of the expert's approach in support of the TNMM. The ATO did not appeal the decision.

SNF Australia (2011)

SNF Australia, a subsidiary of a French global company, made continuous losses for several years. SNF Australia imported industrial chemicals from its parent company and other subsidiaries. The ATO argued that SNF had not established a comparable uncontrolled price, so that it, the ATO, was justified in substituting a profit-based method to arrive at a transfer-pricing determination. A single judge, whose decision was upheld by eight judges on a full bench of the Federal Court, said that SNF had established a CUP and that the payments made on that basis had not exceeded the arm's-length price.

This meant that, despite the ATO's preferred use of TNMM, it was henceforth obliged to use the far more realistic CUP method.

APPENDIX C

A partial list of tax havens

- Andorra
- Antilles
- Austria
- Barbados
- Belgium
- Belize
- Bermuda
- British Virgin Islands
- Cayman Islands
- China
- Costa Rica
- Cyprus
- Delaware
- Dutch Crown Colonies
- Fiji
- Gibraltar
- Guernsey
- Hong Kong
- Ireland
- Isle of Man
- Jersey
- Jordan
- Lebanon
- Liberia
- London
- Luxembourg
- Macau
- Malaysia
- Monaco
- Nauru
- Netherlands
- Panama
- Puerto Rico
- Samoa
- Seychelles
- Singapore
- Uruguay
- Zug, Switzerland

APPENDIX D

Transfer-pricing legislation in Australia

There is a substantial body of relevant legislation and opinion in the *Income Tax Assessment Act 1936* (*ITAA*) and ATO Tax Rulings that comprise the commissioner's view of the law. Section 136AD deals with international dealings, and Division 13 of Part 3 of the *ITAA* covers Australia's law in relation to transfer pricing.

New Sub-Division 815-A allows the ATO to consider transfer-pricing cross-border dealing back to 2004–05. Its retrospectivity is a vexed issue for many free-market-minded thinkers and ethicists. There is always the possibility of unfair or unethical misuse of such legislation to revisit situations where taxpayers were acting on the basis that the law enabled them to act so.

While that is true in most situations, tax is in a different category. On some occasions the damage to national revenue may be so egregious and the behaviour so damaging to the revenue of a nation that retrospective legislation remains the only available defence of the nation's welfare. It is probably the only available remedy for the damage to the national revenue that has occurred in the past 25 years, and the only safeguard for the future. It might make multinationals moderate their behaviour.

It is really not good enough for the finalisation of a major government revenue and payment outcome to be so far away in time on a matter that needs to be resolved and that has implications for other taxpayers and future government revenue. Companies cannot operate efficiently in a market when they don't know whether a profit for a past year, audited and signed off by the ATO, will be reopened and take years to reach a point of judicial resolution (during which years some of the senior tax officers involved who should be witnesses may retire). This drawn-out and inefficient process is likely to cost both the multinational affiliate and the ATO millions of dollars.

The rulings are the ATO's view of the law. They are not the law, but are substantial interpretations that are ignored at the multinational taxpayer's peril. The ATO will generally follow a ruling unless it is persuaded that the ruling has been overtaken by the effluxion of time or a contradictory court decision that is not appealed.

APPENDIX E

Treasury scoping-paper comments

Treasury (under Neil Motteram, principal adviser, International Tax and Treaties Division) issued a scoping paper on 1 November 2011, as part of the consultation process for its review of Australia's transfer-pricing rules. Some of the comments in that paper are relevant for any analysis of the ATO's approach to transfer pricing. The ATO is one of the 20 substantial Australian government departments and agencies that fall under Treasury's broad ambit of policy management and direction.

Treasury notes that the general aim of transfer-pricing or cross-border profit-allocation rules is to ensure 'broad parity between the tax treatment of multinational enterprises and businesses that operate entirely domestically'.

It continues: 'These rules need to be sufficiently robust to protect the Australian tax base — but they also need to be balanced so as not to overreach or impose transaction costs which may inhibit Australia's international competitiveness.'

The paper then notes that trade within companies (that is, among parents and subsidiaries) is 50 per cent of Australian cross-border trade. It is likely that this share has increased substantially since 2011. Most of the growth identified by Treasury is in interest payments, insurance, and services. The paper also notes that the financial value of this trade had doubled in seven years. Treasury also notes that, 'in practice, profit methods are frequently relied upon by taxpayers and administrators alike', and that 'the TNMM is the most widely used method'.

The report predates the outcomes in the Roche and SNF cases, and notes that 'determining an arm's-length allocation of profits is heavily information driven and in a great range of cases much of that information may be peculiarly in the hands of the multinational group' (Para. 74).

The report also notes the recommendation of the Ralph inquiry for a legislative requirement to maintain contemporaneous documentation, as is required in the US and Canada.

Finally, the report suggests a maximum period of between two and four years for completion of a compliance audit. That certainly has not been achieved in major ATO audits. It is not always achieved even in advance-pricing arrangements, which are the ATO's flagship for mutual co-operation between the ATO and a taxpayer that wants future certainty about ATO outcomes.

The report notes that Australian treaties include a provision not included in the OECD documents, for a maximum time limit of eight years, subject to negotiations, on the tax authorities' power to adjust profits. This condition originated in the Japanese agreement, and is reflected in Australia's most recent tax treaties. Treasury states that Australia will continue to propose this in treaty negotiations.

The policy decision seems to have been overtaken by the passage through parliament in September 2012 of the retrospective legislation that has allowed the ATO to reopen Chevron's tax audits for the years back to 2004. No other government has introduced the eight-year rule.

APPENDIX F

The UK parliamentary report on the Big Four

On 26 April 2013, the UK House of Commons Committee of Public Accounts issued its report on the transfer-pricing practices of the Big Four accounting firms. Its report is entitled *Tax Avoidance: the role of large accountancy firms*, and is available at: www.publications.parliament.uk/pa/cm201213/cmselect/cmpubacc/870/870.pdf

This major study clearly shows the huge problems created for mature, large governments by the sheer amount of money and power that multinationals have available to enable their transfer-pricing strategies. The committee's composition and comments demonstrate that there was no party-political motive for its conclusions. It was simply intent on finding the facts and consequences of transfer pricing in the UK.

Official Summary

Confidence in our tax system can only be maintained if every company and every individual is seen to be paying their fair share of tax. We held hearings last year to investigate why some multinational companies pay little corporation tax despite doing a large amount of business in the UK, and why some individuals can get away with using contrived schemes to avoid tax. We are also concerned about the role of tax advisers and in January 2013 we took evidence from Deloitte, Ernst & Young, KPMG, and PwC to understand more about the nature of the tax advice they provide.

HM Revenue & Customs (HMRC) appears to be fighting a battle it cannot win in tackling tax avoidance. Companies can devote considerable resources to ensure that they minimise their tax liability. There is a large market for advising companies on how to take advantage of international tax law, and on the tax implications of different global structures. The four firms employ nearly 9,000 people and earn £2 billion from their tax work in the UK, and earn around $US25 billion from this work globally. HMRC has far fewer resources. In the area of transfer pricing alone there are four times as many staff working for the four firms than for HMRC.

We were pleased that the four firms agreed with us that international tax rules are out of date and need to change to reflect the reality of modern business. Modern communications mean companies need as little as a computer and a handful of staff to set up a place of business in a tax haven. Under current tax rules, this can be enough to establish that they can pay their tax there, rather than where the business activity takes place. This is unfair to responsible companies based in the UK who do pay their fair share of tax. We welcome the Government's commitment to reforming international tax laws, but this will be a lengthy process and, until it happens, we are concerned that companies will continue to find ways to avoid paying tax where they actually do business.

We believe that simplicity is key to fighting tax avoidance. The four firms agreed with us that tax law is too complex and a simpler system is in everybody's interests. It is disappointing that HM

Treasury's Office of Tax Simplification is working with fewer than six full-time staff and as a result has so far focused on abolishing unused tax reliefs, rather than being able to take a more radical approach to simplifying tax law.

Removing unused reliefs may be good housekeeping, but it does little to tackle the problem of complexity and does not prevent the continued abuse of some tax reliefs, such as those to encourage investment in films or donations to charity. We intend to examine those tax reliefs that are widely used and may be subject to abuse at a future hearing.

The four firms insisted that they no longer sell the type of very aggressive avoidance schemes that they sold 10 years ago. While this may be the case, we believe they have simply moved to advising on other forms of tax avoidance which are profitable for their clients; such as the complex operating models they offer to major corporate clients to minimise tax by exploiting the lowest international tax rates.

The four firms have developed internal guidelines on where the line between tax planning and aggressive avoidance lies, but these principles do not stop them selling schemes with as little as a 50 per cent chance of succeeding if challenged in court. Clearly HMRC has to consider the risk to the taxpayer of a protracted legal battle. It would appear that firms and tax avoiders are taking advantage of the constraints under which HMRC is obliged to operate. Furthermore, HMRC is always constrained by resources.

The close relationship that the four firms enjoy with government creates a perception that they wield undue influence on the tax system which they use to their advantage. They told us that they second staff to government to provide technical advice on changes to tax laws and that this has improved the quality of legislation. The witnesses conceded that this may give the perception that they are able to influence legislation to help their larger clients to the disadvantage of smaller UK businesses.

More worryingly, we have seen what look like cases of poacher, turned gamekeeper, turned poacher again, whereby individuals who advise government go back to their firms and advise their clients on how they can use those laws to reduce the amount of tax they pay.

Since our hearing HMRC has announced that it is consulting on a set of draft rules to allow departments to ban tax-avoiding businesses from being awarded government contracts.

This is a step in the right direction, but the draft rules as they stand are narrowly focused and would not cover those companies providing tax advice. The draft rules would allow firms to win government contracts while also advising on schemes that allow their clients to avoid tax. We will want to monitor closely what rules emerge from the consultation process and how they are applied.

Conclusions and recommendations

1. The UK tax system is too complex and needs to be greatly simplified.
2. It is not clear where firms draw the line between acceptable tax planning and aggressive tax avoidance.
3. It is inappropriate for individuals from firms to advise on tax law and then devise ways to avoid the tax (the four firms second staff to HM Treasury to advise on technical issues in drafting legislation). The firms maintained that their involvement had improved the quality of legislation but the concern is that the very people who provide the advice then go on to advise their clients how to use those laws to avoid tax.

HM Treasury should ensure that the code of conduct proposed for tax advisers sets out how conflict of interest should be managed when a firm advises government on the formulation of tax law and subsequently provides tax advice to clients on related areas.

4. The four firms agreed that tax laws were out of date and needed revising. International tax rules have not changed to reflect the way businesses operate globally and through the internet.
5. It is too easy for companies to exploit these rules by setting up structures in low-tax jurisdictions rather than pay tax where they actually conduct their business and sell their goods and services.
6. Greater transparency over a company's tax affairs would increase the pressure on multinationals to pay a fair share of tax in the countries in which they operate.
7. HMRC is not able to defend the public interest effectively where its resources are more limited than those enjoyed by the big four firms. For instance HMRC has 65 transfer-pricing specialists; the Big Four firms have around 250.

   Government must ensure that HMRC is properly resourced to challenge the advice given by the Big Four firms and their offers to companies and individuals seeking aggressively to avoid tax.

APPENDIX G

The OECD

The OECD is the international arbiter for transfer pricing and for tax treaties. It has a difficult task, but has a six-decade history of substantial research; sophisticated, experienced, and knowledgeable staff; and a substantial content database that makes it a formidable champion of the arm's-length standard.

That is not to suggest that it will easily overcome the clandestine (and sometimes open) hostility from the multinationals. The multinationals (supported by the Big Four) are not friendly towards the arm's-length standard; meanwhile, the OECD opposes the multinationals' use of tax havens and the sheer power they exert around the world. The Big Four have certainly expressed a negative public view of the G9 and G20's attitude towards BEPS in the Australian press.*

---

* See, for example: 'Multinationals gear up for a PR attack on tax', Nassim Khadem, *The Age*, 19 June 2015, http://www.theage.com.au/business/comment-and-analysis/multinationals-gear-up-for-a-pr-battle-on-tax-20150618-ghr1is.html; 'Define a tax haven, business lobbies tell government', Nassim Khadem, *The Age*, 23 June 2015, http://www.theage.com.au/business/the-economy/define-a-tax-haven-business-lobbies-tell-government-20150622-ghui6a.

The OECD is not interested only in BEPS. A major task of the OECD Global Forum, with its 122 member-nations, is to audit and rate the standards for tax transparency in the OECD's member countries. Among them are several countries that are regarded as tax havens. The forum reviewed 50 national jurisdictions in 2013, some of which (for example, Bermuda, the Cayman Islands, and Jersey) are known as tax havens. Only a few were determined to be non-compliant (Seychelles, the Virgin Islands, and, partly non-compliant, Turkey).

The Global Forum has a major role in reviewing tax treaties, which has been and will continue to be one of the most important areas of OECD review over the next decade. Some people regard treaties as opportunities for tax avoidance, but they have great importance in that they are aimed at preventing the double taxation of both parties over any transaction that involves two or more countries.

In Australia, in the past, when multinational affiliates were moving towards an annual profit level that would make them subject to company tax of 29 per cent, the usual strategy was for the affiliate to contact the regional office and organise an invoice for intellectual property, interest, manufacturing knowledge, or any other of the fees that multinationals may charge their affiliates if it fits their transfer-pricing strategy. The accounts would only be paid when it fitted the global strategy, and the payment would attract tax deductions for the subsidiary.

It has taken the OECD over 20 years to move aggressively against transfer pricing and identify the fundamental threat it has become to the global economy. That pace is simply too slow. The damage to national tax collections has been immense. If the Big Four have been paid $US500 billion in 25 years, how much tax have their multinational clients avoided globally? It must be in the trillions of dollars.

The OECD has always had the authority to delay membership until a government corrected or at least committed to correcting financial accounting and taxation peccadilloes in their country. I suppose it would have been impossible to exclude the United States, as the OECD is largely a US creation. However, transfer pricing is not the US government's fault. Barack Obama has spoken out strongly about the failure of US multinationals to pay a fair share of their income as tax.

In May 2007, the OECD invited excluded countries to open membership discussions. Chile, Estonia, and Israel joined in 2010. Russia was offered open discussions for membership. Brazil, China, India, Indonesia, and South Africa are still waiting.

In 2014, the OECD and Europe were agreed on the damage done to economies by transfer pricing. There has been no overt dissension yet from the US. Both the G9 and the G20 have come out strongly against BEPS. The likely alternative may be to begin a process of changing bilateral and multilateral agreements in relation to tax rates on specific functions, assets, and risks. These agreements often relate to concessional tax rates on intellectual property, loans, and manufacturing knowhow.

Charter and date of establishment

The OECD was established on 30 September 1961. Senior public-service oriented, it could be the big brother of the Australian Treasury, the Reserve Bank, and the old Diplomatic Corps within Foreign Affairs. Its annual budget is €400 million ($A606 million). It has 2,500 staffers in Paris and other staff establishments exist in major countries. Again, it is similar to the old Diplomatic Corps embassy approach. It services members and non-members alike, and has an extensive, unmatched library on global trade.

OECD Action Plan

We know what the OECD plans to do, but will have to wait until later in 2016 for it to spring into action. In the meantime there has been a lot of commentary from both the OECD and the Big Four in relation to the OECD Action Plan.

Some good 'pro-global' changes have already been made. The OECD has an excellent methodological approach to the conduct of its global work and the delivery of its objectives.

It flows as follows: data collection; analysis; discussion; decisions; implementation; peer reviews; and multilateral surveillance.

This process is inclusive, intelligent, and sensitive. There is a need to tread softly in an environment where the failure to pay the tax that should be paid means that the taxpayer will be seeking (except where they finish up in a tax haven) to recover tax from what is often the multinationals' home market. Correlative relief is obviously morally correct, but it often takes a long time for the home tax authority to give some of the money back.

Glossary

This glossary is a preliminary resource for understanding the technical terms used in taxation and transfer pricing.

Ad Valorem Tax

A tax on goods or property expressed as a percentage of the sales price or assessed value.

Advance pricing arrangement

An arrangement that determines, in advance of controlled transactions, an appropriate set of criteria (for example, method, comparables, and appropriate adjustments thereto, critical assumptions as to future events) for the determination of the transfer pricing for transactions over a fixed period of time. An advance pricing arrangement may be unilateral, involving one tax administration and a taxpayer, or multilateral, involving the agreement of two or more tax administrations.

Arm's-length transaction

A transaction in which two unrelated and non-desperate parties agree to a price.

Base erosion and profit shifting (BEPS)
The term 'base' refers to a company situated in a low-tax or non-tax country (that is, a tax haven) that is used to shelter income and reduce taxes in the taxpayer's home country. Base companies carry on certain activities on behalf of related companies in high-tax countries (for example, management services), or are used to channel certain income, such as dividends, interest, royalties, and fees.

Big Four
The world's four largest accountancy firms, which handle the vast majority of audits for publicly traded companies, as well as for many private companies: PricewaterhouseCoopers (based in the UK), Deloitte (US), Ernst & Young (UK), and KPMG (Holland).

Big Eight
The ancestors of the Big Four: Arthur Andersen, Coopers and Lybrand, Deloitte Haskins and Sells, Ernst and Whinney, Peat Marwick Mitchell, Price Waterhouse, Touche Ross, and Arthur Young.

Chinese walls
A barrier that separates two or more groups within a single enterprise, usually as a means of restricting the flow of information.

Comparable Uncontrolled Price (CUP) Method
A method used to determine if the prices reported in a related-party transaction are comparable with prices for similar goods and services in an arm's-length transaction. This method relies on a direct comparison of prices, and is applicable only when the goods and services are capable of being sold in an open market.

Correlative Relief

When a tax authority in a second country adjusts a transfer price upwards, the tax authority in the home country makes a corresponding adjustment downwards, thereby providing the home-country taxpayer with 'correlative relief' — that is, a negotiated partial refund of the money originally paid by that taxpayer.

Cost, Insurance, Freight (CIF) Valuation

When duties and taxes are assessed on the sum of the product value, the shipping cost, and the insurance cost.

Cost Plus

A transfer-pricing method using the costs incurred by the supplier of property (or services) in a controlled transaction. An appropriate cost-plus markup is added to this cost, to make an appropriate profit in light of the functions performed (taking into account assets used and risks assumed) and the market conditions. What is arrived at after adding the cost-plus markup to the above costs may be regarded as an arm's-length price of the original controlled transaction.

Current Domestic Value

The amount for which the seller of the goods to the purchaser in Australia is selling or would be prepared to sell for cash, at the date of exportation of those goods, the same quantity of identically similar goods to any and every purchaser in the country of export for consumption in that country.

Customs duties

Duties on goods imported into a country.

Dumping
A form of predatory pricing, especially in the context of international trade. It occurs when manufacturers export a product to another country at a price either below the price charged in its home market or below its cost of production.

Float
The term refers to the regular shares that a company has issued to the public that are available for investors to trade. This figure is derived by taking a company's outstanding shares and subtracting from it any restricted stock.

Free-trade zone
A specific class of special economic zone, this is a geographic area where goods may be landed, handled, manufactured, or reconfigured, and re-exported without the intervention of customs authorities. There are over 6,000 free-trade zones around the world.

G9
Canada, France, Germany, Italy, Japan, Russia, Great Britain, the United States, and the European Union.

G20
The G20 is made up of the finance ministers and central bank governors of 19 countries: Argentina, Australia, Brazil, Canada, China, France, Germany, India, Indonesia, Italy, Japan, Mexico, Russia, Saudi Arabia, South Africa, South Korea, Turkey, Great Britain, and the United States. The remaining seat is held by the European Union, which is represented by the rotating European Council presidency and the European Central Bank.

Harmonised Tariff System

The Harmonised System (HS) is a broad classification system of about 5000 six-digit headings which are used for classifying goods involved in international trade. It has been adopted as the basis for describing and classifying goods for customs purposes by most trading nations. HS eases the process of making products comparable.

Model Tax Convention (Treaty)

A model tax treaty is designed to streamline and achieve uniformity in the allocation of taxing rights between countries in cross-border situations. Model tax treaties developed by the OECD and the UN are widely used, and some countries have their own model treaties.

Resale Minus

This transfer-pricing method begins with the price at which a product that has been purchased from an associated enterprise is resold to an independent enterprise. This price is then reduced by an appropriate gross margin (the 'resale price margin'), representing the amount out of which the reseller would seek to cover its selling and other operating expenses and, in the light of the functions performed, make an appropriate profit. What is left after subtracting the gross margin can be regarded, after adjustment for other costs associated with the purchase of the product (for example, customs duties), as an arm's-length price for the original transfer of property between the associated enterprises.

Tax Haven

A country that is used by corporations to avoid tax which otherwise would be payable in a high-tax country. Tax havens have the following key characteristics: the imposition of no tax or only nominal taxes; lack of effective exchange of information; and lack of transparency in the operation of legislative, legal, or administrative provisions.

Transactional Net Margin Method (TNMM)
A transfer-pricing method that ostensibly uses the net profit margin relative to an appropriate base (for example, costs, sales, assets) that a taxpayer realises from a controlled transaction. In reality, this is a self-serving technique, by which means multinationals use the lowest comparable cost they can find as a basis for declaring their taxable income.

Transfer pricing
The price charged by a company for goods, services, or intangible property to a subsidiary or other related company. Abusive transfer pricing occurs when income and expenses are improperly allocated for the purpose of reducing taxable income.

The OECD Glossary of Tax Terms
Several of the definitions above are derived from the OECD's *Glossary of Tax Terms*, which can be accessed here:
http://www.oecd.org/ctp/glossaryoftaxterms.htm